FORWARD

This publication is a chronology of India Battery 3rd Battalion 12th Marines as it details their journey from Hawaii in February 1965 to Vietnam, landing in March of 1965, and terminating in October of 1965 when the Battery Commander Captain Don Harman was transferred. Various other documents from the 65-66 time frame are included. All documents are in the public domain.

John R. Booth, Colonel USMC (Ret)

INDEX

July 8, 2021

BTRY I 3RD BN, 12TH MARINES; CAPT. D. R. HARMAN, CMDG. — 1ST SGT. C. M. ANDERSON — M.C.A.S., KANEOHE, HAWAII, July 21st 1964

3

1. Pierce	31. ~~Walker~~ *Jim Wright*	61. Wade	91. Actie
2. Kijewski	32. _____	62. *Bucher*	92. Anderson
3. Kiker	33. Boehme	63. ~~Mariott~~ *Marliatt*	93. George Cross
4. Bill Baird	34. Wozniak	64. Singleton	94. Bill Schaeffer
5. Hook	35. Huss	65. _____	95. Moon ~~Mullen~~ *Mullins?*
6. Struck	36. Woodhouse	66. Muino	96. McFadden
7. Bliechert	37. Scroggins	67. *Swarthout*	97. Don Harman
8. Billy Smith	38. Falluca	68. Brewer	98. Bill Townsend
9. Foster	39. Clarke	69. _____	99. Jim Beery
10. Bell	40. Pendleton	70. Owens	100. Don Rosenberg
11. Gentry	41. *Terry Summerville*	71. Richardson	101. Carl Satterfield
12. Nelson	42. Wery	72. Donovan	102. Noll
13. Roland	43. Mooney	73. Barno	103. Al Foley
14. Potter	44. *Foster (little)*	74. McClendon	104. Joe Featherstone
15. Pelger	45. Disante	75. Schonhoff	105. Taylor
16. Kobarg	46. _____	76. Sam Dunson	106. Jones
17. Miller	47. Smith	77. Garcia	107. Matafa
18. Bieker	48. Ellis	78. Russo	
19. Smith	49. *Blanchard*	79. Stanker	
20. Closser	50. Marlow	80. Reedus	
21. Norris	51. Powers	81. Kirchoff	
22. _____	52. Seggie	82. _____	
23. Smejkl	53. Carter	83. Fordyce	
24. _____	54. Walker	84. Taylor	
25. Woodall	55. Hannafin	85. Allen	
26. _____	56 _____	86. Guerin	
27. Phillips	57. Domingez	87. Carioty	
28. Tuckerman	58. Griffen	88. Soliasia	
29. Bartelt	59. Jones	89. Oliver	
30. Wade	60. Baker	90. McCardle	

RLT 3

~~3/3~~ 3d Marines
Btry L 4/12
Plt 8

BLT 3/4   3/4E5

3d Bn, 4th, Mar
Det, Hq Bn 3d Mar Div
Btry I (Rein) 3/12
3d Plt (Rein) Co C, 3d Tanks
3d Plt (Rein) Co B, 3d AT
3d Plt (Rein) Co A, 1st Amtrac
3d Plt (Rein) Co B, 3d Recon
3d Plt (Rein) Co B, 3d Engr
Det, 3d Serv. Bn, 1st Mar Brig
Det, Coll Plt, Co B, 3d Med Bn
Det, 3d Dental Co,
Det, 3d FSR
Det, Co B, 3d SP Bn
3d Plt (Rein) Co C, 3d MT

UNITS AND DETACHMENTS OF 3RD BATTALION 4TH MARINES AT PHU BAI IN EARLY 1965

5

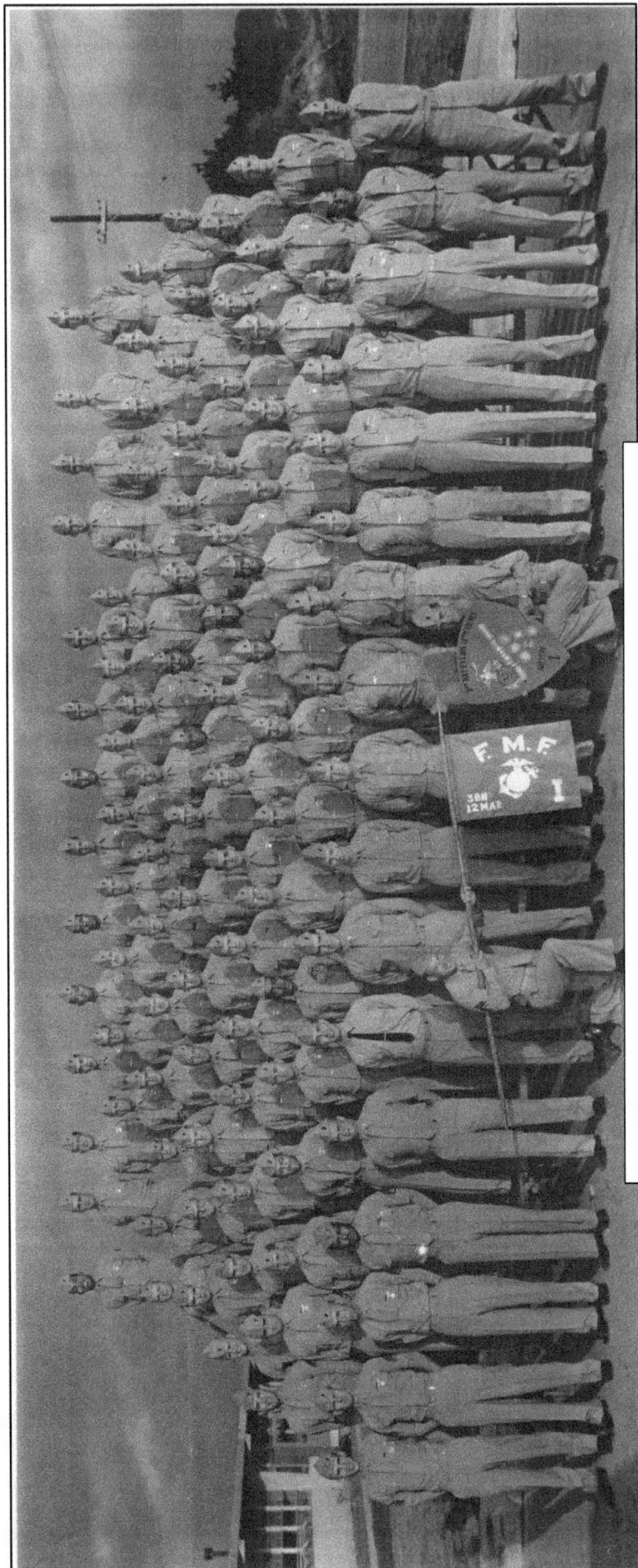

INDIA BATTERY FEBRUARY 1966 CAMP HANSAN OKINAWA

o—o—o

1 August 65 10:30 a.m.
Hue Phu Bai, RVN

Dear Bill,

Just finished reading the Advocate the folks sent me. Thought I would drop a line or two.

Been here for about 4 months now, and really been eating up the culture of this place. Dust usually blows around here so bad you eat a lb. a day, that is if it is not raining. The monsoon season is soon to hit, but I hope to be heading for Okinawa when it does.

I heard that Bob Andera is in the DaNang area. Been trying to get down to see him on my travels to Chu Lai (once or twice a month), but he is usually off and gone somewhere.

I thought that in this note, I would let you have a little look at this place. My unit is based 12 miles south of a city called Hue (pronounced Way). This is the closest unit of ground troops to North Viet Nam. Before here, I was at Hawaii, which was very colorful. Now I must say that Viet Nam is much more picturesque than that Island Paradise. Hue is the oldest city in Viet Nam and once was the capital center of education for V.N. with the oldest college.

We get liberty every once in awhile and can see that the French were here once. Their traits are very dominating, but now the Americans are here. At first they were leery of accepting us, but prosperity will have an effect on anyone.

Little info on my unit. A group of men with a 105 millimeter Howitzer Battery. We can all be proud of our record. Fired well over 6,000 rounds in close to 4 months and have not had a mistake that has caused the life of our own troops. Only artillery in Viet Nam with this distinction. Doing a good job over here and shall continue to until we are relieved. Have had a little aggression from V.C., but no KIA's for our side.

Five men from Iowa are in this unit so it kind of makes us feel at home.

Guard time soon, so I shall stop hen pecking for awhile. Sure did enjoy the paper, and hearing of home. Keep up the good work, always interested in the home town news. Drop a line if you have time.

A Young Wiltonian
LCpl M. G. Woodhouse
BLT 3/4
Btry "I", 3rd Bn., 12th Marines
3d Marine Division (Forward), FMF
c/o FPO, San Francisco 96601

o—O—o

Good luck, Meredith!

Recently received a letter from Meredith Woodhouse, a Wilton serviceman now stationed in Viet Nam. Meredith is the son of Mr. and Mrs. Harold Woodhouse, Wilton. It is always nice to hear from our young men in the service, especially one in a theater of operations we see, hear and read so much about. Thought you folks would enjoy sharing the letter.

Marine's Letter Hits Responsive Chord In Many American Homes

By MSgt. Walter Stewart

Da Nang (USMC-IO) — A Marine's open letter to anti-Vietnam demonstrators in the United States, reprinted by a number of U.S. newpapers, has earned the writer considerable response— all of it favorable.

Lance Cpl. Terrence O. Melton (Phoenix, Ariz.), serving with the 1st Bn., Third Marine Regiment, wrote the letter in July. It first appeared in the pages of the Arizona Republic.

"What you really need is a good spanking," he wrote the demonstrators, "and then come out from behind mother's skirt and have your eyes opened to what the communists are trying to do to the world, and then maybe you will know what we are doing in Vietnam."

Referring to an article about students taking up a collection to help the Viet Cong, he suggested that they "go and ask our parents and the parents of our friends who have lost their lives trying to end the war, to contribute. Then wait until we get home, if we do, and ask us, if you can find the nerve."

The letter hit a responsive chord in a number of American homes.

One mother wrote, "...most of the young Americans who demonstrate against our position in Vietnam are either misinformed, ignorant of the communist threat to our democracy, or afraid of being called in to fight."

A letter, signed by a family of six, said, "We have our nice refrigerated home because someone else is willing to live in a tent and mud to see that we can."

"People here do care," wrote a San Franciscan. "Probably that is why they are so afraid of what the situation really means — afraid for the families broken up by it — afraid for the lives that have been and will still be lost — afraid mostly of what will happen if the aggressors can't be contained, or better yet made to retreat."

From a former Marine: "...those punks are so misguided that they don't even know what's good for them, and too stupid to know when someone is using them."

Marine recruiters wrote that they were reproducing copies of the letter for display and ended with "...give 'em hell!"

Some of the letters were addressed to Melton's mother.

In a mother-to-mother congratulatory note, one woman said, "In comparison to the number of beatniks and nonconformists it seems that there aren't too many young men who have the courage and common sense to express their patriotism and convictions."

Another wrote, "I was proud of the letter your son wrote to those cement heads."

And the mail keeps coming in.

Marines' Big Question: What Will Families Do?

By BOB JONES

PHU BAI, South Viet Nam —In a tent at artillery's I Battery, 11 married men sat around and tried to find some solution to questions about their families back on Oahu now that the Marines think they will be here for a year.

The men were Pfc. John Keuling, Cpls. Ed Bartelt and Paul J. Wilson, Sgts. B. E. Pate, George E. Hodge, Dewey E. Wilder, Jim Green, Al Foley, Thomas McCardle and James Carioty, and Gunnery Sgt. Carl Satterfield, all formerly of Kaneohe Marine Corps Air Station.

Most of them don't know yet what they'll do with their families. Some I've talked to say they will leave them in Hawaii until this tour is up.

"Don't rush your decision," Capt. Don Harman told them. "Write your wives and talk this thing over before you do anything rash."

The Kaneohe Marines have been ashore at Phu Bai since early May, but things haven't really improved much at this hothouse.

Somewhere along the line it was decided the 1st Brigade Marines here could do without the comforts afforded other service organizations in South Viet Nam.

Just 10 miles north of here, in the city of Hue, Military Assistance Command advisers on the Army staff are eating food fit for any restaurant's table.

The day I stopped in, the lunch menu was spaghetti and baked rabbit provencale, choice of salads, unlimited lemonade and ice tea, and apple pie with a slice of cheese on top.

At Phu Bai, the Kaneohe Marines are still eating canned B rations — powdered eggs, salty hash, frankfurters tasting strongly of preservative, and a thick vanilla pudding that most of the men throw in the garbage barrels.

At the Marine regimental headquarters in Da Nang,

See MARINES on A-2, Col. 1

Where To Find It

A SECTION	
Amusements	10, 11
Temperatures	4

B SECTION	
Ann Landers	3
Business and Finance	4, 7
Crossword Puzzle	8
Comics	8
Editorial	2, 3
Radio Programs	4
TV Programs	4
What to Do	8
Your Birthday	8

C SECTION	
Classified Ads	4-15
Ship Movements	16
Sports	1-4

Reporter Jones, right, prepares to move out with a Marine patrol.

8

Marines' Big Question: What Will Families Do?

Continued from Page 1

seat of "government" for the 3rd Division, the fare is A rations — that is, normal food which is served in the chow halls of every base. It includes steak and eggs cooked to order.

At Phu Bai, some Marines have stopped believing there is such a thing as a steak in all Viet Nam.

I asked why the Marines have been called on for this unusual "guard" duty and was told only that the mission is classified.

But Marine sources in Da Nang have said this:

Original plans made at Camp Smith called for elements of the 25th Infantry Division at Schofield Barracks to be sent in as a security force, backed up by the lavishly supplied U.S. Army Support Command, Viet Nam.

The Army is reported to have said it could not commit its forces without first setting up the proper support forces in Phu Bai.

Marine Lt. Gen. Victor H. Krulak said his men were ready to go, support or not, and within days the Kaneohe Marines were called back from Exercise Silver Lance on the California coast and earmarked for Viet Nam.

There are some things about a war that never make any sense, and this one is no exception.

When Gen. Krulak made his 2-hour visit here, brigade troops were called out to present a full honor guard. They had practiced the day before in the sun outside one of the battalion tents.

A spunky corporal, who shall here remain nameless, spoke up for a lot of the Marines when he told Krulak's party he didn't think honor guards should be held in a combat zone.

Captured Viet Cong documents contain orders from Hanoi saying that no intentional combat engagements are to be made with the Marine force. Most of the VC force, Vietnamese Army

Our Man in Viet Nam

The Advertiser's 29-year-old military editor, Bob Jones, is now with Hawaii's fighting men in Viet Nam.

He is the first—and only—newsman whose exclusive assignment is to cover the 1st Marine Brigade from Kaneohe, the Army's 25th Division "shotgun riders" from Schofield and Isle Navymen.

JONES

intelligence officers say, have pulled back across the Ta Trach river, the limit of the brigade's fighting zone.

But to keep up the heat-wilted morale of the troops, patrols are still made across the barren foothills which are visible in any case to the Marines manning the hilltop observation posts.

Every war produces a few soldiers who — for better or for worse—will stick out in the unit as the memorable characters.

Two of these in this dusty guerrilla war are Maj. James Conrado Jr., the battalion operations officer, and Capt. Harman, commander of I Battery artillery.

Conrado could probably win a popularity contest, hands down. He's got a wife back in Hawaii like many of the men, but he's one of the guys who has his heart with the dirt-eating leathernecks.

Said he: "I guess I've always believed in the Marine Corps. I'm not one of those savior-of-the-world types. I believe in the system — that the system will weed out the 10 per cent of the bastards you're bound to find in uniform.

"I've never made any mistakes that were fatal to anyone, but I've made a couple that I regret."

Conrado gets only about five hours of sleep a day and sometimes it puts an edge on his personality.

"I chewed out four lieutenants — two of them that deserved it and two of them

who were just young learners and I didn't explain to them what they had done wrong. In other words I really didn't help them at all."

Harman, whose wife Joan is with the current University of Hawaii graduation class in education, is the "can-do Charlie" of the outfit.

When there isn't a drink to be found in any tent or foxhole, Don Harman is the man who can rustle up a Texas fifth of gin—which he doesn't mind sharing with his driver and back-home babysitter, Cpl. Lester E. (Skip) Marlatt.

Where most captains command a battery for no more than a year before being transferred into staff jobs, Harman has had one for 58 months.

"I don't care. They don't want any part of me on that staff and I'm happy out here."

"Out here" is his battery tent, far away from the battalion, where he runs the outfit with a cool hand.

He is fond of calling his enlisted men "sir," and he keeps three goats grazing outside the tent from which he surveys the battery guns.

"Let us never forget, gents," he told his NCOs recently, "that this damn Marine Corps is a form of insanity, and you have to be a little insane yourself to get along in it."

The little bit of insanity may be what will keep the Kaneohe Marines going these days in the heat and the upcoming monsoon rains.

JUNE 1965
PHU BAI, VIETNAM

Battery "I", 3rd Battalion, 12 Marines

CHRONOLOGY

Date	Action
11 Feb 65	Personnel dropped to Sub-Unit #1 : 2 Officers-6 Enlisted
12 Feb	Vehicles staged for embarkation
15 Feb	USS Oak Hill LSD-7 Loaded Battery vehicles (less TD-18) at KMCAS. Embarked 1 Officer and 21 enlisted personnel. USS Ft. Marion LSD-22 Loaded Battery TD-18 and 1 enlisted man.
16 Feb	USS Oak Hill LSD-7 Moved to Pier K-7, Pearl Harbor. USS Ft. Marion LSD-22 Moved to Pier K-11, Pearl Harbor; 3 enlisted men embarked.
17 Feb	USS Paul Revere APA-248 Embarked 8 enlisted men at Pier W-4 Westlock. USS Calvert APA-23 Loaded 2 liaison vehicles and 2 drivers at Westlock.
19 Feb	USS Oak Hill LSD-7 Moved to Pier F-9, Ford Island, Pearl Harbor. Debarked 4 enlisted men.
20 Feb	USS Calvert APA-23 Disembarked 2 enlisted drivers; vehicles remain aboard.
21 Feb	USS Paul Revere APA-248 Embarked 8 enlisted men at Pier F-13, Ford Island.
23 Feb	Personnel dropped to Sub-Unit #1 : 1 Officer-2 Enlisted
4 March	Personnel joining from Sub-Unit #1 : 1 Enlisted
8 March	All ships put out to sea at 1115 with the following number of troops embarked:
9 March	Ships returned to Ford Island, Pearl Harbor, at 2030.
10 March	Personnel dropped to Sub-Unit #1 : 1 Enlisted Personnel joining Battery "I": 1 Officer-1 Enlisted

8 March troops embarked:

	Officers	Enlisted
Oak Hill LSD-7	1	17
Paul Revere APA-248	0	16
Calvert APA-23	0	0
Ft. Marion LSD-22	0	0

Date	Action
11 March	0030- Troops embarked on Oak Hill and Ft. Marion. 0730- Remaining troops departed KMCAS and were aboard ships by 10000 as follows:

	Officers	Enlisted
Oak Hill	3	55
Paul Revere	2	55
Calvert	4	14
Ft. Marion	0	1
Total:	9	125

1430- All ships departed Ford Island, Pearl Harbor...
Destination unknown.

26 March

USS Paul Revere APA-248
    Debarked 2 Officers-55 Enlisted, and unloaded equipment at Naha, Okinawa.

USS Calvert APA-23
    Debarked 4 Officers-14 Enlisted, and unloaded equipment at Naha, Okinawa

27 March

USS Oak Hill LSD-7
    Debarked 3 Officers-55 Enlisted, and unloaded equipment at White Beach, Okinawa.

USS Ft. Marion LSD-22
    Debarked 1 Enlisted and unloaded equipment at White Beach, Okinawa. Motor march to Camp Sukiran
    All troops billeted at Bldg. 490, Camp Sukiran.

28 March   Battery "I" designated as artillery support for SLF 3/4.

1 April   Battery "I" redesignated as artillery support for BLT 3/4(rein)

2 April   Personnel dropped to HQ 3/12:
    19 Enlisted

3 April

Joined from HQ 3/12 : 10 Enlisted
Joined from "H" Btry: 2 Enlisted
Joined from "G" Btry: 2 Enlisted
Joined from 4.2 Btry: 2 Enlisted
Joined from NGF SFCP:

USMC	USN
1 Officer-11 Enlisted	1 Officer

5 April

Following units attached:
    Co."A" 1st Amtracs:

USMC	USN
1 Officer-46 Enlisted	1 Enlisted

    Co."B" 3rd Anti-Tank Bn: 1 Officer-24 Enlisted

    Co."C" 3rd Tank Bn. 1 Officer-23 Enlisted

2

Date	Action
6 April	Battery "I" inspected by C.O. 3/12, and C.O. BLT 3/4.
7 April	Vehicles staged at White Beach; 23 Enlisted moved to White Beach.
8 April	18 Enlisted moved to White Beach.
9 April	2 Enlisted moved to White Beach; all equipment loaded.

10 April — Remainder of Battery "I" (-) Rein. moved to White Beach and embarked as follows:

USS Vancouver LPD-2 :

	USMC		USN	
	Officers	Enlisted	Officers	Enlisted
Battery "I" (-)	4	102		2
Co."A" 1st Amtrac	1	46		1
Co."B" 3rd AntiTank	1	24		
Co."C" 3rd Tank Bn	1	23		
NGF SFCP		1		

USS Henrico APA-45

	USMC		USN
	Officers	Enlisted	Officers
NGF SFCP	1	10	1

USS Henrico departed White Beach; destination...Vietnam

Date	Action
11 April	USS Vancouver departed White Beach; destination;..Vietnam
12 April	Designated as Artillery support for CTG 79.5 ; Troops received initial briefing on objective...Hue Phu Bai.
13 April	Final preparations made and briefings held.

14 April — USS Vancouver LPD-2
    Debarked 1 Officer and 3 Enlisted (C.O.w/recon party);
    Amphibious landing at Red Beach #2, DaNang.
    Helilifted to BLT 3/4 HQ at Hue Phu Bai.
    Battery "I" HQ established ashore, C.O.'s recon carried out.

Uss Henrico APA-45
    Debarked 2 Officers and 10 enlisted from NGF SFCP.
    Amphibious landing at Red Beach #2, DaNang
    Helilifted to BLT 3/4 HQ at Hue Phu Bai.

15 April — USS Vancouver LPD-2
    Debarked 1 Officer-32 Enlisted. All personnel and equipment transported by LCVP's and LCM's up SONG HUE RIVER. Landed at Hue, motor march to BLT 3/4 HQ at Hue Phu Bai.

16 April — Debarked 25 Enlisted and 6 howitzers. Troops and guns transported up SONG HUE RIVER as on 15 April. Guns arrived at 1600, battery laid and ready by 1700, registration conducted at 1840...1st round from 1st Marine Brigade fired in South Vietnam.

3

Date	Action

16 April   "B" Company, 3rd Antitank Bn.(1 officer and 24 enlisted) detached.

Briefing by Gen. Throtmorton; Battery C.O. attended.

30 enlisted retained on Vancouver to provide ship's platoon.

Ass't Ambassador Johnson and party of three toured battery area; escorted by Battery C.O.

Lt. Henderson sighted one VC armed near Post #2.

17 April   NGF returned to Battery "I"; 1 ship available, NGF on call.

1 M422 "Mighty Mite" deadlined with clutch out, sent to FSR; all other combat essential equipment in good order.

2 enlisted debarked from Vancouver.

and Col DUPRAS

Col. Wheeler, RLT 3 C.O. toured battery position. Advised Battery C.O. that guns and equipment are prime VC target. Priority of work: local security and outpost fortification.

Gen. Westmoreland briefed by BLT 3/4. Lt. Schaeffer represented Battery "I".

Liaison and communication established with ARVN. Cpls. Marlatt and Little to advise and participate in nightly ARVN shoots outside BLT 3/4 TAOR. Capt. Bao--C.O. of 12th ARVN Artillery.

Battery "I" mess will also feed Company "L", B-Med, and Tank Platoon; augmented by 5 cooks and messmen accordingly. B-rations expected to go into effect 25 April.

Tanks occupy flank of Battery position. Mission: 1) illumination 2) indirect fire 3) mobility for infantry.

Survey to battery position (Arty/Tanks) completed.

LtCol. Nielson (FSCC 9th MEB) visited battery.

18 April   Easter Sunday (no Easter eggs)
16 enlisted debarked from Vancouver.

Chaplain Lane held outdoor services.

LCpl Holifield's vehicle hit by rifle fire during supply run from Hue to Hue Phu Bai...2 tires shot. In the excitement of the occurance, Holifield accidentally discharged his .45, thus wounding himself in the thigh. Lt. Bartels investigating. Holifield should return to Btry in 10 days; recovering at DaNang hospital.

Date	Action
18 April	PFC Smith, G.R. collided with Vietnamese civilian who was riding bicycle. Claims officer notified.
	Night illumination mission fired for Company "L".
	Outposts encountered small arms fire; excited the complete battery, negative casualties.
19 April	Infiltrators spotted and fired upon by Post #2 and tank #2.
	PFC McEvoy fired upon 3 times while driving from Hue to Hue Phu Bai. Truck hit, tire blown. Pfc Barno fired upon two minutes later while driving the same route.
	1 officer and 17 enlisted debarked from Vancouver. All Battery personnel ashore.
20 April	LtCol Slack, 3/12 C.O., visited battery position.
	1 squad from Reconnaisance Platoon stationed in rice paddies in front of tank position to ambush night infiltrators... no contact made.
	Battery C.O. made trip to Hue to attend briefing, reference TAOR. Col Wheeler USMC (RLT 3), Col. Bissett USA, and Brig. Gen. Chung ARVN. Agreement reached that TAOR would be expanded.
21 April	All gun positions dug in. Work will be done on continued improvement of positions.
	Battery C.O. held meeting with Capt. Young, Army advisor. Discussed local situation, and role and employment of artillery in the area.
22 April	UPI and API pressmen and photographers escorted through battery position and briefed by Battery C.O.
	12th Artillery (ARVN) reinforced first USMC artillery mission.
	Battery daily fires check rounds on R.P. and fires on call missions.

5

Date	Action
23 April	Lt. Bartels flew to DaNang in regards to Holifield investigation.

1 Marine from 3/4 on outpost accidentally killed himself and wounde 1 other Marine when fragmentation grenade exploded in his hand. *[handwritten annotation]*

Platoon size group of VC spotted on outskirts of TAOR by Recon. Illumination fired by ARVN. Battery "I" continues to fire on call illumination missions.

24 April — LtCol. Jones evacuated with heart seizure, relieved of BLT. New C.O.--LtCol. W.W. Taylor.

Afternoon registration conducted.

Reception in Hue for BLT 3/4 and 9th MEB. General Chung host. Guests of honor...Gen. Karch and Col. Wheeler. Capt. Harman, Lt. Henderson, GySgt Anderson, and Sgt. Green represented Battery "I"; trip made by helicopter.

Recon patrol encountered VC on edge of TAOR; 2 Marines killed, 5 wounded. Battery "I" fired close artillery support. Fired 44 rounds(illumination, WP, and HE). First definite VC KIA's in Vietnam by USMC artillery unit confirmed, one of which was brought back to BLT area for intelligence gathering. Had map on him pin-pointing our artillery position. *[handwritten annotation]*

This battery has settled down; reaction time on mission... 3 minutes. Battery "I" has gained the respect and confidence of the infantry units due to its fast, accurate support fires. Personnel of battery now realize that its Vietnam junket will not be a holiday.

25 April — 1st meal served from Galley...Sunday morning brunch.

Church services outdoors held by Chaplain Lane.

Registration conducted; gun drills held.

LtCol. W.W. Taylor talked individually to each Company C.O., and to Artillery C.O., Capt. Harman.

6

Date	Action
26 April	Registration conducted. On call missions fired.
27 April	Major JOHNSON, USA, senior Artillery Advisor, I Corps, discussed 12th ARVN reinforcing role.
	Lt. SCHACHT joined Battery. Assigned F.O. "K" Company.
	Concentration fired in.
	Greatest amount of outpost activity thus far encountered. No casualties.
	General quarters drill held.
	PFC TUCKERMAN joined Recon as Arty F.O.
28 April	Gen. Wallace Green, Commandant, USMC, visited BLT 3/4.
	36 heat casualties from "Mike" Company. Concentration fired.
	Lt. Col. TAYLOR toured outpost area; recommended position changes of posts #1 and #2. Recommendations "hesitantly" complied with.
	Major WATSON, BLT 3/4 X.O. spent the night in Battery area.
	12th ARVN Artillery held farewell party for Sgt. MARLOW, Army Advisor. Capt. HARMAN, GySgt. SATTERFIELD, Sgt. WILDER (NGF), Sgt. HODGE, and HM1 FRANCIS represented Battery "I".
29 April	PFC TUCKERMAN evacuated from hill...suspected spinal meningitis.
	Lt. SOECHTIG moved out to occupy Hill 180 as Arty F.O. with NGF Spot Team and Radar Beacon Team.
	GySgt. SATTERFIELD accompanied Capt. YOUNG to 12th ARVN battery positions in DaNang area.
30 April	Two platoons from "India" 3/4 stationed around battery perimeter in anticipation of VC May Day Activities. No incidents.
	Triple strand concertina barbed wire began around perimeter.
	PFC TUCKERMAN evacuated to Tachikawa, Japan. Condition guarded Doctor KILLINGER suspects blood disease(thrombocydopedia).
1 May	Cpl. LITTLE went with Recon as Arty F.O. to Hill 225. Did excellent job firing in concentrations.
	Battery defensive fire plan, indirect minimum range fire capabilities submitted to BLT 3/4.
	Liaison made with 8th RRU. for availability of 8 81mm Mortars. Results affirmative..

7

Date	Action

1 May — Lt. Col. TAYLOR and Artillery C.O., Capt. HARMAN, toured perimeter and established barrage data for Battery "I", and 81 Mortars.

2 May — Intelligence dictated two VC Battalions massing in Southern portion of TAOR. Division Artillery through A.O. requested Battery "I" and 12th ARVN to displace 2000 meters forward to Hill 180 to fire indirect observed fire on target. BLT C.O. gave permission. Battery "I" fired 450 rounds as reinforcing unit, with 12th ARVN adjusting unit. Surveillance: secondary explosions and undertermined number of casualties. Reaction time: 1000-warning order; 1015-orders passed to X.O. and FDO to move battery out with 450 rounds of ammo and occupy position by Hill 180; 1110-1st rounds fired (Battery 5). (This was Battery "I"'s first "liberty" since occupying position. Well done by all hands.)

3 May — LCpl BOEHME and Cpl LITTLE accompanied Recon. Received small arms fire at 0130 and pulled back to line companies' perimeter.

"Kilo" and "Mike" companies fired upon infiltrators. Post #3 fired upon moving object near barbed wire. No positive identification made.

Continued work on concertina and field fortifications.

4 May — 2 reinforced squads from "Mike" Company to take up fire-team sized positions between Battery "I" outposts in inner perimeter. New orders for outposts: after dark, do not challenge, do not illuminate, and shoot to kill anything moving in front of positions.

5 May — Registrations conducted, and concentrations fired in.

SSgt. JOHNSON requested mast with LTCol. TAYLOR.

Target area survey complete. Registration conducted. FDC switched from observed to surveyed fir chart.

6 May — Continued liaison with ARVN. Nightly, a Vietnamese Artillery Officer spends night at Battery "I" FDC with Lt. BEERY.

Lt SCHAEFFER and Lt. CROSS made Artillery liaison to DaNang; delivered Artillery, NGF, and Air Fire Plans.

Normal routine: on-call missions.

Plague shots given to Battery.

Ammo expended as of 6 May:

HE	WP	ILLUM	TI	VT
708	58	19	27	102

8

Date	Action
7 May	Cpl. LITTLE and Cpl. MARLATT accompanied Recon to Hill 225. Fired Battery 6 on suspected VC buildup. Village chieftain reported 21 VC killed.
	ARVN artillery fired reinforcing mission for Lt. ROSENBERG; reaction time slow, but good effect.
8 May	Capt. HARMAN and Lt. HENDERSON accompanied inspecting party to two ARVN artillery outposts at A Luoi and A Shan, near Laos. Inspecting party consisted of Maj. JOHNSON, USA, Capt. YOUNG, USA, Capt. BAO, ARVN, and GySgt. VANCE, USMC. Both outposts in bad state of repair, however, their airstripes are in fairly good shape. Outpost at TaBat destroyed by U.S. and ARVN because of inavailability to man all three outposts effectively. Outposts remotely located in valley near Laos near dense, nearly impassable jungle. Very little artillery firing done... one 105 howitzer per outpost.
	Intensive night fire-fight near roadblock. Two tanks and 1 platoon from "L" Company dispatched. No Marine casualties, no VC bodies recovered. Battery "I" fired continuous illumination.
	Cpl. LITTLE spent night on Hill 225 with 1st Platoon, "Kilo" Company. Received 14 rounds of incoming 81mm Mortar; reported same to FSCC. All rounds were 200 to 400 meters short. No casualties.
9 May	On call missions fired.
	Steak fry for Battery "I" Officers at Capt. HARMAN's tent. BLT 3/4 X.O. was not invited, but showed up unexpectedly.

9

DATE	ACTION
10 May	LtCol. TAYLOR and Capt. HARMAN held a discussion in the CO's tent on artillery tactics and their application to the present situation with the following results:

a. The battery will have a central location and will rove by echelon to selected positions in order to support operations throughout the TAOR, returning to the central location at the completion of the said operation.

b. An OP was established forward of Phu Bai, Airfield.

c. All FO's will be maintained in a pool, remaining with the Battery until attached.

LCpl BOEHME established an OP on hill 225, and Cpl. LITTLE accompanied Recon as an FO. Lt. WALKER, FO for "I" company returned to the battery area.

Item of Interest: 155mm Howitzers from 12th ARVN artillery fired three rounds within 100 meters of "I" company's perimeter, and Lt. WALKER's FO team.

Battery continues to fire on call missions and H & I fires.

| 11 May | Lt. SCHACHT and Lt. ROSENBERG returned to the battery area to debrief CO. Both FOs have been utilising split FO teams, and this tactic has proved quite successful. Lt. ROSENBERG returned action of 12 KIAs inflicted by this battery.   ESTIMATED |

General KARCH and party toured the battery area. The General's remarks were that this is the best laid out artillery position he had seen in VietNam.

| 12 May | Lt. SOECHTIG and team returned from hill 180 to be replaced by Lt. HENDERSON. There has been little activity from hill 180, but the BC scope has been very effective in that position. |

The following permanent OOPs have been established as of this date:

a. Hill 180   Lt. HENDERSON
b. Hill 225   Lt. WELD
c. Airport   Lt. SCHACHT

It is expected that Lt. WELD will have considerable activity in his location.

The battery has been granted liberty in Hue to use the swimming pool there. Liberty is from 1200 to 1700 and is on a percentage basis.

10

CHRONOLOGY OF EVENTS 11-15 MAY 1965

~~TI 4 DIARY~~ — ~~LIWELD~~

DATE	ACTION

11 May   Departed airfield 0730 arrived hill 225. Immediately established 3 OP's in order to have continuous observation 6400 around hill 225. Gave my my binoculars to one OP so that all OPs would 7-50's established My OP at BC scope. Had Cpl. LITTLE brief me concerning terrain features and conc. locations. Observed no movement all day. 1600 fired conc. 610 to observed max. range. Made a terrain sketch nothing all key terrain features and observed fire concentrations. Informed all night time OP's to be particularly watchful for Mortar flashes or sounds.

12 May   Continued 6400 observation. Was particulary watchful from 0530 to 0700, but no contact. Suntan 3 arrived hill 225. Observed no movement all day. AT 1715 Suntan 3 wanted me to fire WP into wooded area on rigde line vicinty of hill 220. Adjusted rounds into wooded area, excellent effect on target, but no fire. Shifted left 500, but still negative fire. At this time TPS-21 observed a target coming over ridge approx 1500 right of last volley. Converted degrees to mils and sent TPS-21 range. First rounds directly on line and just short of contact. Total darkness, so completely depending on TPS-21. Illum not deemed practical due to range (3500m) and scrub growth. After first volley contact began retreating at rapid rate. Added 400 and rounds where just over causing contact to change direction again and come back toward us. Dropped 200 and TPS-21 observatio said volley was directly on target, causing some troops to disperse in all directions. 10 minutes later TPS-21 picked up target again AT same range AND moving to left. Shifted left 150 and again rounds on target. Troops made a hasty retreat over ridge line and lost contact. Conc. 611-fire Conc. 612-TPS-21.

13 May   0500 began observing diversionary fire. S AT 0730 Recon and M-2 flushed 8-VC in draw at base of hill ~~225~~ 163. Could not observed at this time due to ridge line. 0740 saw 3 VC run up out of THE draw across base of 163 and into wooded draw, running OP 163. Requested Suntan 3 let me shoot over M-2 and to the right of Recon. Suntan 3 asked me if I could do it without hitting Recon ~~and~~ or M-2. M2 was 300m short of draw and Recon was 200m to the lef Told Suntan 3 affirmative and he gave me O.K. First rounds landed top of draw. Dropped 100 and brought rounds down to middle of draw. R 50-100 brought rounds to exact point were 3 VC were suspected to be. RR, fire for effect. Outstanding sheaf all 6 rounds in draw. Shell mixed, RR, R fire for effect. Again all 6 rounds in draw, RR RFFE. Again all 6 rounds in draw, EOM to allow M-2 to survey draw. M-2 moved one squad rapidly through found nothing. Believe survey not through enough (Conc. 613). Decided to take advantage of Btry displacement and fired across river. Recon had observed VC on trail 3 times. Adjusted conc. on trail and shifted to greater range to cover THE draw to rear. TI-4A fired conc. 615 on village to support Recon's withdrawal. From this position effect on target appeared excellent.

PAGE 1 of PAGES 2

~~ENCLOSURE 1~~

Enclosure (2)   11

20

DATE	ACTION

13 May   AT 1715 spotted 4 VC moving into treeline. 3d adjustment ^GAVE direct hit on tree line. 3 VC starting running to the left. Gave shift of 500 left to try to cut them off. Received "Cease Fire" from TI-22 air on station. 10 minutes later received my volley. Again saw 3 VC running to left; shifting left 500 and was on target just as VC entered wooded draw. FFE; good sheaf all 6 rounds in draw; RR, RFFE; again good effect. 10 minutes later observed 1 VC wandering around in front of draw. Shifted R50-100 and saw VC go into cave on side of draw. Could see opening and VC 'on ^IN CAV LEFT 20 RR brought right round of two rounds right smack into cave opening. Estimate 1 KIA and possible 2 WIA. Conc 616 - recommended Conc. 614, 61 & 616 for H & I fires.

14 May   Continued 6400 observation had no contact until 1700 when I spotted 7 VC (4 armed 2 carrying large objects- possibly Mortars or Ammo) moving into wood line where I spotted the 4 VC last night - vicinity RPG. Battery had to return to airfield leading me to believe that ^WAS the reason for the 600 left I received when I requested L 100. Shifted to the right and 2 volley on line 50 meters over. Gave D 50 FFE. During time interval 5 VC started running to left. Just as I was going to give a shift left, received on the way. FFE on target, excellent effect. Shifted left to catch VC in open. VC ran behind a little knoll and I adjusted VT on top of their suspected position. At this time Suntan 6 stopped my mission." "If you haven't got them by now, you never will." I would like to have given one more shift to flush ^THEM out from behind the knoll. Possibly WIA's or KIA's because VT was right on top of their suspected position. L-3 moved to approx. area and saw 1 VC moving slowly out of area ^BUT could not pursue because of fading light. Suspect WIA.

15 May   Requested fire mission to have FFE data on woodline for possible future contact ~ refused!

DATE	ACTION

13 May   On this date Battery "I" with companies "L" and "M" and the Recon platoon participated in an operation to reconnoiter the area around hills 225 and 163 extending to the Ta Trach river in order to prepare the area for future operations. While there were no definite indications the enemy's strength and no sightings of VC units larger than 10 men, the enemy was, nevertheless, believed to have the capability of massing units up to battalion size.

At 0545 Battery "I" displaced by echelon to a new position across the Khe Can Thu river. The first echelon was in position by 0610, the second arriving at 0630. A registration was fired immediately upon arrival of the second echelon and was completed at 0657. At 0730 the battery fired diversionary fires in conjunction with ARVN artillery. The first enemy target, 6men in the open, was taken under fire at 0740. Surveillance of the area fired upon was accomplished by units from the Recon platoon who found one weapon and a pair of shoes there. In addition, bloodstains were found on trails leading from the area indicating that casualties were inflicted although the number could not be accuratly estimated. At 1135 a mission using shell mixed was fixed at an area of possible enemy activity. This was coordinated by the battalion commander. No surveillance was possible. At 1153 "M" company FO called a mission on a VC village, but this had to be suspended until 1300 due to cease fire for air evacuation of a VC prisoner. The mission was continued at 1305 and completed at 1315, resulting in extensive damage to the village. Between 1330 and 1720, the battery experienced little activity. At 1720 a fire mission was called on 3 enemy in a tree line, but was also interrupted by a cease fire for air craft in the area. At 2016 the battery began to fire H & I fires. At 2050 a mission was fired on suspected enemy activity. Four VC attempted to pentrate the battery perimeter at 2328, but were discovered and repulsed by machine gun fire. H & I fires were completed at 0535.

A contingent of about 20 men remained in the battery CP location to provide local security for that area. Two squads from "K" company assisted in this mission which was accomplished without incident.

General COLLINS and Colonel WHEELER visited 3/4 and received a briefing on the operation.

14 May   Battery "I" remained in position throughout the morning and early afternoon to support "L" company and portions of "M" company in the destruction of Thuong Phuong village which was accomplished without incident.

During the morning, one light and one heavy section of tanks with three Ontos proceeded to Thuong Phuong village to supply and provide transportation for "L" company. However, the armored force

13

DATE   ACTION

- 14 May   encountered approximately 20 VC in a woodline where the terrain was such that the tanks could not give pursuit. There were no personnel casualties on either side as a result of this incident, but the Ontos suffered damage to two recoiless rifles as the result of bullets entering the bores.

At the completion of the operation, the battery returned by echelon to the CP location, the first echelon arriving at 1610. While enroute a fire mission was sent by Lt. WELD from hill 225 on 8 VC in the open. Lt. BARTELS reacted swiftly with the first echelon to begin the adjustment. While the adjustment was in progress, Lt. BEERY arrived with the second echelon, bringing his guns into position in time to fire a battery two rounds. The result of this quick reaction and coordinate was four enemy KIAs.

The success of any operation must be attributed to the personnel involved, and this one was no exception. While it is not possible to name every individual involved, the following men should be singled out for recognition:

    Lts. BARTELS and BEERY whose efforts as battery executive officer and FDO contributed greatly to the success of the operation.
    Lts. CROSS and ROSENBERG, FOs for "L" and "M" companies respectively, who took part in the destruction of Thuong Phuong village.
    Lt. WELD, also with "M" company, who, from his position on hill 225, did an outstanding job of adjusting and observing fires.
    Lt. HENDERSON who observed fires and maintained a communacations relay for the battalion from hill 180.
    GySgt. SATTERFIELD, who did an excellent job in the battery position.
    Cpl. LITTLE, FO with Recon platoon, who took part in the capture of two VC.

As a result of this operation, the infantry claimed 1 KIA, 1 WIA, and 2 prisoners, while the artillery claimed an estimated 8 KIA. In addition to the personnel casualties inflicted (none were received) the following material was captured or destroyed:
    1 village, Thuong Phuong, with accessories
    1 VC wounded - later died
    1 VC captured - later died??
    2 VC rifles, MAS 36, 7.62mm
    600 lbs rice
    3 cane knives
    25 rds of 7.62mm ammo
    1 ammo pouch and belt and U.S. poncho
    13 flashlight batteries
    2 packs candy
    Assorted cooking utensils and rice bowls
    1 pair sandals
    3 pair trousers
    Assorted clothing
    1 flashlight

14

DATE	ACTION
15 May	As a result of the past two days operations, there has been a lull in the TAOR.

General CARL paid a visit to 3/4 and expressed the possibilty of PCS as of 1 July.

The morale of Battery "I" remains at a high level. At present all hands are preparing for a visit by General KRULAK on 18 May.

| 16 May | Holiday routine was observed within the battery with church services being held outside the CO's tent at 1000. |

Liberty was granted in Hue to the battery on a percentage basis. Battery "I" was alloted a quota of seven men. Selection was made on a merit basis from these individuals not having office hours in their records. Liberty will not be granted to these individuals who do have office hours. The following men were granted liberty:

    LCpl BOEHME
    PFC STAMEY
    LCpl WERY
    PFC MOONEY
    SGT WILDER
    CPL PATTI
    CPL BAIRD

The consensus of opinion was that Hue is an interesting city, and all hands enjoyed the liberty. There were, as expected, no un-fortunate incidents involving Battery "I" personnel.

At 1700 the battery fired a concentration called in by Lt. WELD from hill 225

At 1800 hours Capt. HARMAN held a steak fry at his tent for the Battery "I" officers. Officers attending were Lts. BARTELS, BEERY, ROSENBERG, WALKER, SCHACHT, and SOECHTIG. Lt. AHEARN, S-2 for 3/4 also attended. Special guests were LtCol. TAYLOR, CO of 3/4, Captain BAO, battalion commander from the 12TH ARVN artillery, and Mr. Bob JONES from the Honolulu Advertiser. Mr. JONES is visiting VietNam in order to do stories on brigade personnel here.

High point of the evening was the presentation of a gold tie clasp to Captain BAO making him an official Marine "Cannon-Cocker". Capt. BAO has been in the Vietnamese Army for almost 12 years having graduated from their military academy in 1954.

15

DATE   ACTION

17 May   Lt. WELD returned with his FO team from hill 225 and briefed the CO
          on the operation of 13-14 May. Lt. WELD then spoke to the battery
          in order to give the men a first hand account of the effect the
          artillery has been having. The context of Lt. WELD's speech is
          enclosed.

          Throughout the day, Battery "I" continued preparations for General
          KRULAK's visit, improving the road through the battery position
          to accommodate the General's convoy.

          At 2127 the battery conducted a reinforcing mission forward of Phu
          Bai village for the ARVN artillery at the request of Captain BAO,
          because the target area was out of range of his 105mm howitzers.
          This was an action rear mission using fuze VT. The battery fired
          6 rounds in adjustment and a battery 4 rounds in effect. The mis-
          sion had been called to the ARVN artillery by the village chief of
          Phu Bai village on suspected VC activity, and the ARVN platoon
          which conducted the surveillance, ▄▄▄▄▄▄▄▄▄▄▄▄▄▄▄▄▄▄▄▄▄
          ▄▄▄▄

18 May   At 0820 General KRULAKs arrived at Phu Bai airfield to begin his
          visit with 3/4. First on the itinerary was the inspection of the
          honor guard which included a squad from Battery "I" under Sgt.
          WILDER. Other members of Sgt. WILDER's squad were: Cpl. PATTI,
          LCpl RABLEE, LCpl SMITH, PFC DAVIS, Cpl. FORDYCE, LCpl. WERY, LCpl
          BOEHME, PFC SHARP, Cpl. GUMTO, LCpl MARLOW, PFC MOONEY, and PFC
          SWARTHOUT. After the inspection of the honor guard, which he said
          was outstanding, the General was briefed at RRU by the CO of 3/4
          and the CO of RRU. At 0915 General KRULAK arrived at Battery "I"
          for a briefing by Captain HARMAN and a tour of the battery area.
          Captain HARMAN requested 10 promotions to LCpl from the General
          and will receive some portion of that amount. After a tour of the
          airfield area, the General flew to hill 180 where he was briefed
          by Lt. HENDERSON. At 1000 he completed the visit and departed
          Phu Bai for DaNang.

          After the General's visit, the Battery observed holiday routine.

                                                                        16

Date	Event

19 May — Today was Ho Chi Minh's birthday. The battery had planned to celebrate by holding a surprise party for some of Ho's friends, but they didn't show up.

LCpl Marlow killed a four foot, yellow and black striped king snake in the battery area. The snake was not poisoness.

At 2130 the battery fired another reinforcing mission for the ARVN Artillery at the request of Captain BAO. As with the previous reinforcing mission, this one required action rear. The reaction time was four minutes. The mission utilized only one platoon which fired two rounds of VT, and then switched to illumination, firing 6 rounds. The target was a VC platoon in the rice paddies forward of Ha Thuong Village near the East Lagoon. Three VC were killed, one of them in the act of throwing a hand grenade.

Between 1700 and 1800, the battery fired concentration data for Lt. Schacht, FO with "K" company.

20 May — At 0630 the battery fired concentration data on two more targets for Lt. Schacht. A total of four rounds were used.

At 1030 four rounds of base ejection smoke were fired at RP 7, North of Phu-Bai airfield. Base ejection was used instead of the normal HE for possibly hitting civilians. This was the first time the battery had fired on that side of the airstrip. Sgt McCardle did the survey of the area while Captain Harman performed the duties of FO, and as a result of this combination, all four rounds landed within 50 meters of the target. There were, however, a couple of interesting and unusual aspects to this mission. The first was that the battery fired at an elevation of 84 mils. This in itself would not be unusual except that the Exec's computed elevation was 72 mils, and a little simple arithmetical computation will show only 12 mil clearance. However, Captain Harman has never been one to worry excessivly over minor details so long as the rounds clear the deck and hit the target, which they did in this case. The same cannot be said of the village chief of Chan Tau who became upset - even alarmed - at what he thought were duds scattered about within his area. The civilian populace also seemed somewhat indignant over the nine people they thought had been killed. Nobody could explain how three duds could kill nine people when it is difficult to get that kind of effect even with VT, but apparently the question never came up. Nevertheless, with world diplomacy and international relations being as they are, the matter had to be cleared up all the way from Dong Da down to Chan Tau. The final result of the whole affair was a summit conference attended by Captain Harman, LtCol Taylor and the village chief to explain that the artillery had fired in the area only to show the VC that it could be done, and that the shells were smoke cannisters and not duds. This pleased the village chief, and appeased the civilian populace. However, it is doubtful that the VC were either pleased or appeased.

17

Date	Event

20 May   "L" Company moved their bivouac area from Phu-Bai airfield to a position adjoining post #2 within the battery perimeter.

The battery now feeds the following units within its mess:

    Major Watson, executive officer for 3/4
    B-Med
    Tanks
    Line Company which is guarding the airfield perimeter.

21 May   Today Battery "I" participated in another operation similar to that of 13-14 May. The mission was again one of reconnaissance, this time of the Thuong Phuong Village and the east-west ridgeline in that area. While a platoon size force is the largest unit the VC was expected to be able to mass in this area, Company or Battalion size units could be massed west of the Song Ta Trach.

Battery "I" had the mission of supporting the reconnoitering force which consisted of Companies "I" and "K" and the recon platoon. To help support Battery "I" in this mission there was a 2 gun platoon of ARVN 155mm Howitzers and 2 UH-IE gun ships with AO's.

The battery displaced by echelon to Khe Cam Thu in the early morning hours, the first 3 guns leaving at 0515 and the second 3 leaving 15 minutes later. The entire battery was in position by 0610.

At 0756 the battery fired its first mission which was called in by Lt. Schaeffer on a suspected enemy position. 18 rounds of HE and 15 of WP were fired with a good effect on the target although casualties could not be estimated. The mission was completed at 0830. Forty minutes later the AO, Lt. Weld, called in another mission on a suspected enemy mission, and the battery fired 8 HE and 6 WP, again with good effect on the target. Lt. Weld fired a second mission at 0947 on a similar target with the same results.

Lt. Weld and Lt. DeForrest, the "M" Company CO were the two AO's.. Lt. DeForrest had been an AO previously and chose Lt. Weld to accompany him on this operation because Lt. Weld was familiar with the concentrations plotted in the area. While on the operation Lt. Weld's plane received small arms fire, and was hit twice. They fired back using machine guns and rockets with an effect described by Lt. Weld as "looking like WW III".

At noon Cpl Marlatt, who was with the recon platoon, called in a mission on a suspected enemy position. This target was out of range of battery "I" and had to be taken under fire by the ARVN 155's.

18

Date	Event

21 May   The mission was interrupted by a cease fire for air in the area. At 1300 Cpl Marlatt called in another mission, this time on an enemy bunker, and this too had to be fired by the ARVN Artillery. The bunker received 2 direct hits and although casualities could not be estimated it can be assumed that the occupants of the bunker did not survive the ordeal.

At 1500 the battery received the order to displace by echelon and return to base camp, the first echelon arriving at 1530. The second echelon arrived a half hour later. The fact that this operation did not have the volume of activity of the former one, is an indication of the success the BLT has been experiencing in the past couple of weeks.

At about 0900, message #200646Z arrived from RLT 4 informing BLT 3/4 the PCS orders had been approved effective 25 May. When the Battery returned from the operation Capt. Harman informed the men of this fact. The news was received gracefully if not with enthusiasm. Then the Capt held a meeting of married personnel to discuss special problems that may arise. None are anticipated with the possible exception of automobiles shipments.

Major Gibney and Captain Miller paid a visit to the battery at about 1000. They had an opportunity to inspect the battery position, and to discuss with Captain Harman any problems that may arise concerning 3/12. They departed at 1530.

The battery has been continuing to grant liberty in Hue with the quota being raised from 7 to 13 men. The basis for selection of personnel has not changed. Battery "I" continues to set the example for 3/4 by having no problems with personnel on liberty. In addition the battery was permitted to send one man to Saigon for a three day R&R period. Sgt Tompkins was chosen for this detail.

22 May   Lt. Soechtig accompanied a heavy section of tanks on a patrol to the area near Phuoc Lam Village on the edge of the TAOR. One of the tanks broke an oil line and had to be towed back. As a result of this casualty the patrol could not return to base camp before darkness and had to spend the night in the field.

Shortly after noon the battery fired a WP marking round on hill 207 for an air strike. 2 A4D's ~~but~~ the area with napalm and rockets.
HIT

19

DATE	EVENT

22 May   The men of Battery "I" got their first close look at the enemy today. A truck from the battery was dispatched to Lang Xe Village to recover the bodies of two VC who had been killed by the Engineers. The bodies were then brought to the battery area so the men could have the opportunity to see them. The sight was a sobering if not pleasant one. After exhibition, the VC were turned over to the ARVN.

23 May   The battery observed holiday routine with church services being held at 3/4 at 1000 and at B-Med at 1130. Breakfast included fresh eggs which were the first "A" rations that have been served. The menu for evening meal included steak with all the trimmings. All personnel who have had the opportunity to compare the mess at Battery "I" with that at 3/4 concluded that the Artillery is by far the better of the two.

24 May   Fresh eggs were again on the breakfast menu which also included donuts.

Liberty runs to Hue continue daily with liberty now being granted to Officers. Lt. Soechtig was the first Battery "I" Officer granted liberty.

LtCol. Brooks, regimental Executive Officer acting CO in the absence of Col. Wheeler visited Battery "I"'s area. He was accompanied by LtCol. Blanchard and Major Browse. The visiting Officers were particularly impressed by the gun emplacements and the galley.

20

DATE	EVENT

25 May
to
30 May

During the past week, there has been enough work within the battery area to keep everyone occupied. The line company which has the responsibility of guarding the airfield now mans post #2 on the battery perimeter . This change was made because the company now lives in the same area in which post #2 is situated. They also provide flank security for the areas between posts #1 and #3.

Two additional observation posts, designated O1 and O2 have been established forward of Phu-Bai airfield. Post O1 is manned by Battery "I" and reinforced by personnel from motor transport. Post O2 is manned by the 81mm Mortar Platoon. Sergeant MC CARDLE did the survey for both OP's.

Lieutenant BEERY has devised a counter-mortar board to facilitate obtaining firing data on critical terrain and it is expected that this will be utilized from the new OP's.

On Saturday and Sunday the battery FAM fired all personal weapons and Machine Guns.

Captain HARMAN has submitted a letter to Lieutenant Colonel TAYLOR requesting that counter-mortar radar be provided for the battalion. He also recommended that the howtar battery be attached to 3/4.

Corporal MARLATT has returned from exile and has been reinstated as the CO's driver.

As of this date, the VD rate for battery "I" has been zero. Whether or not this is to be attributed to self-control, prior planning, or just plain good luck cannot be accurately stated. It shall suffice to say that we stand on our record.

Liberty continues for Battery "I" after a slight interruption caused by two erring individuals from 3/4.

Lieutenant SOECHTIG relieved Lieutenant HENDERSON on Hill 180, and Lieutenant WALKER remains on hill 225, activity from both OP's has been slight.

The battery has also had a large number of visitors during the past week. General COLLINS paid a visit to the BLT to bid farewell as he is scheduled to leave the 3d Marine Division. The former Brigade Commander, General Youngdale, visited the 8th RRU and took the opportunity to tour the battalion area as well. Colonel GARRETSON RLT 3 Commander, also toured the area and was particularly impressed by Lieutenant's BEERY's counter-mortar board, the gun emplacements and, of course, the ever-popular Battery "I" galley. The galley seems to be as much an item of interest and symbol of artillery as the guns. Not all of the visitors have been military. Mr. Joseph O'NEAL, the American Consul from Hue, spent Saturday night in the battery, and was treated to a steak dinner with all the trimmings. Major WATSON was also a welcome guest at this steak fry especially since he provided the steaks and trimmings which included two quarts of gin.

2/

DATE	EVENT

25 May
to
30 May
Cont'd

Military activity within the TAOR has not been great although the VC provide enough nightly entertainment to keep things interesting. Most of the firing has been H&I missions.

On Friday the battery commander reconnoittered forward positions across the Song Ta Trach. The recon party included eight men, an M-422 and an M-35. The area was not the relativly open Viet Nam with which we have become familiar in the past month. Instead, this was the Viet Nam of the stories and books which we had expected to find. The air was heavy and damp with humidity and the ground smothered by dense vegetation. The still waters of the river cut a black path through the surrounding jungle. This was the land of the Viet Cong as evidenced by the 57mm recoiless rifle shell and the 81mm mortar cannister found there. Eight rounds fired at the party from hill 153 gave even more convincing evidence that unfriendly people dwell in the area.

On Sunday Capt. HARMAN and Lieutenant ROSENBERG made another recon to the area of hill 96 to select positions for a forthcoming operation.

The fact that there has been little activity within the TAOR is no indication that the VC are getting less active. They are merely changing the area of their operations. It seems almost as if they are aware of the limits imposed by the TAOR and are purposly avoiding it.

Two APC's were destroyed near Phu-Bai village which is just outside the TAOR, and 1 ARVN Officer with 18 enlisted men were killed. The Battery fired illumination during this activity. Farther north, near Hue, the railroad was sabotaged and partially destroyed for the first time in this area. The largest action, and also the worst defeat, occurred at Mang Ca about 14 Km South of the TAOR. Here an outpost of about 100 ARVN troops and two 105mm howitzers were over-run by the VC. There were no survivors reported. As a result of this, an ARVN battalion departed from Phu-Bai airfield by helicopter on Sunday to reestablish the position.

There have been reports of an even larger defeat involving an entire battalion, but so far there has been no official information concerning this.

22

DATE	EVENT

31May65   At 0530, the battery displaced by echelon to a forward position in order to support an infantry exercise. The guns were in position, laid, and ready to fire by 0650. The position was in an area known as the oasis, so called because of a growth of palm trees and an abundant water supply from the nearby river. The river was deep enough that all hands could enjoy a swim call although a leech watch had to be maintained on the banks, the water being infested with these parasites. This marked the greatest penetration into the TAOR yet made by the artillery battery, and the necessary local security was furnished by the ontos platoon.

"K" Company had performed a reconnaissance in the area of hill 336, and found definate signs of the VC. However, the area was a dense jungle, consisting of double canopy tree growth sometimes reaching a height of 150 feet, and this made artillery fire ineffective with the exception of fuze delay. The company was able to locate one VC in this area, and fired upon him but the enemy escaped into the underbrush. The problem secured at 1800 and the battery returned to base camp by echelon.

While the preceeding operation was in progress, the base camp also experienced some action in the form of small arms fire in the Battalion CP. Although patrols were sent out to locate the source of the shooting no contact was made, and it was believed that a single VC delivered the fire and escaped into Phu-Bai Village.

1Jun65   The battery has been making preparations for the CO's inspection on 5 June.

W.O. Jones, the division postal officer, paid a visit to the battery to discuss the mail situation. Mail delivery in the past has been something less than satisfactory with unacceptable delay in the receipt of mail. However, the gunner gave assurance that the situation will improve in the near future.

A picture was taken of all Battery "I" Officers and Staff NCO's. Moustaches have become so much in style, one could almost believe that all hands are anticipating the Lahaina Whaling Spree.

The June draft departed today on a one hour notice, but no complaints were voiced by those departing. Battery "I" lost the following 11 men: Pfc BARTLETT, LCpl BLEICHERT, Pfc CLARKE, Cpl CULVER, Sgt FOLEY, LCpl NOBLE, Pfc NORRIS, LCpl PARRIS, Pfc PEIGER, Pfc SCHULTZ and Pfc STAMEY. This was an excellent group of men and will be missed by the battery.

Big time sports came to Viet Nam as Battery "I"'s volleyball team defeated 81mm mortars.

Battery "I" 105mm howitzers fired a battery 3 rounds on Phu-Bai

23

DATE	EVENT

1Jun65   village for ARVN Artillery and also fired illumination for recon with Cpl Little acting as FO.

2Jun65   Liberty in Hue was granted for the first time in 8 days. The rest of the battery made preparations for a visit by General Walt who succeeded Gen. Collins as 3rd Marine Division Commander.

At 1310 "K" Company received 8 rounds of mortar fire and Cpl Lang called in counter mortar fire. There were no casualties from the mortars. Lt. Weld accompanied the reactionary force sent by "M" Company to assist "K" Company and his helicopter received small arms fire. No damage was done.

Captain Bao of the 12th ARVN artillery requested a helicopter to evacuate an officer from Nan Wan.

Outpost 01 which was recently established forward of Phu-Bai airfield came under attack. It was estimated that 6 to 8 VC with automatic weapons fired on the outpost. When asked how many rounds were fired the radio operator was heard to reply "I don't know; I was hiding". There were no casualties as a result of this incident.

3Jun65   Preparations were completed for the visit by General Walt and General Westmoreland. The generals visited 3/4 but did not tour the battery area. One result of this visit is the possibility that an RLT with an 8 in howitzer platoon may be sent to Phu-Bai in the future.

8 Stars were in the area this date - Gen Westmorland, Walt, Kier, Fontana, and McCutchin.

4Jun65   At 1200 the battery was given an order to displace three guns to a position near Lang Xa village. The purpose of this move was to support a reaction force which had located a platoon of VC hidden in a draw. Lt. Bartels and Lt. Beery accompanied the forward elements while Lt. Cross and Lt. Rosenberg remained with the rear. The movement was accomplished in 37 minutes with all three guns being laid and ready to fire in that time. The rapid movement was largly the result of the SOP written by Lt. Bartels. The FDC planned 54 missions on suspected enemy positions and fired 15 of them. The battery remained in position until 1800 and them returned. Lt. Welds "Payable "I" 4" (Payable India is the new call sign) diary gives an account of the success attained by the infantry which prompted the S-3 to say "It's good someone other than artillery is killing".

24

PAYABLE INDIA – 4 DIARY
4 JUNE 1965

1045 – Received word from Mike Company that the Alert Platoon was being committed.

1049 – Heli-Lifted from Battery Area to vicinity Coord 817108 near hill 69 where a squad from India Company had contact with a VC Platoon.

1100 – Arrived area and observed 1 VC KIA from initial contact with India Company. Before helo's had left 1 more VC came out of a swampy draw and surrendered. At this time I believed the action to be over and chose a vantage point from where I could observe all exits from the area in an attempt to cut off any VC fleeing from the area.

1115 – From top of hill 69 observed entire area but saw no VC continued to observe until 1130 and returned to contact scene where a sweep of the draw was beginning.

1145 – Mike-2 began to sweep top of draw while India started on the bottom. Mike-2 took incoming rifle and AR fire and hand grenades but no casualties. Mike-2 threw hand grenades into the hole followed by rifle fire and a search which reveiled 3 very dead VC. Mean while India Company was having equal success at the bottom of the draw killing 1 VC and wounding another.

1220 – The terrain was rugged in the swampy draw and movement was difficult at best. M-2 flushing two more at the head of the draw and India Company one at the bottom made us believe that we were on to something really big. 3 more KIA's

1245 – The captured VC was brought back to the scene to point out the location of 2–60mm Motars and 2 Machine Guns. An extensive search only yielded 1 Machine Gun. The search continued as the sweep progressed through the draw. M-2 discovered still 2 more bushy hideouts which resulted in 3 eventual KIA's.

1330 – Engineers arrived with a mine sweeper in an all out attempt to find the motar tubes. The search uncovered a weapons and ammo storage. 7–60mm rounds w/fuzes and ignition cartriges were found along with 10 hand grenades of various sorts and sizes.

1400 – Montitored conduct of fire net and heard the battery conducting a fire mission against 2 Platoons of VC called by an AO. Heard 2 adjustments and then FFE. The effect on target must have been good due to short time interval.

1430 – Still another pocket of VC was discovered and M-2 accounted for 2 more KIA's

25

34

1600 - A thorough search of the surrounding area yielded 2 well camoflouged Platoon size bases.

1700 - An after operation count yielded the following:

- 1 POW
- 1 WIA
- 13 KIA
- 1 Light MG
- 5 AR's
- 3 rifles
- 2 Carbines
- 7 60mm rounds
-10 Hand Grenades
- 1 Large medical kit
- Serveral large clothing packs

1700 - I continued to search the draw in one last attempt to find the VC motars. Was unable to do same. It is my belief that the tubes were thrown into the bottom of one of the deep pools.

1745 - Returned to Base Camp for debriefing by Captain Harman.

1930 - Was alerted for operation tomorrow.

5 JUNE 1965

0600 - Heli-lifted to draw between hill 163 and hill 153 as a blocking force for a sweep by Lima Company, India Company, and Recon.

0610 - Circled in Helicopters while the battery preped the LZ. Observed excellent effect on entire LZ with fuze VT.

0615 - Landed and took vantage to observe draw. Sent two fire missions to seal-off any escape routes but missions were canceled by Mortgage 3.

0630 - Continued observation until 1330. Sweeping units made no VC contacts.

1400 - Returned to Base Camp for debriefing by Captain Harman.

26

PAYABLE INDIA-4 DIARY

7 June 1965

- 0700 - Heli-lifted to Coord 878048. Requested Check Round on Conc. CI-215 - Mortgage-3 Canceled Mission.

- 0915 - Arrived Coord. 892070 and Fired Mission, Conc. 630, on Avenue of Exit From Stream Bed. 2 Plts were beginning their Sweep toward This Point.

- 0945 - Requested Check Round on Conc CI-217, But Had to End Mission Because a Squad Had Wandered Out of its Area and was Headed Toward the Impact Area.

- 1015 - Requested Check Round on Conc CI-215 - Mortgage-3 Canceled Mission.

- 1615 - Sent a Registration Mission within 100m of Conc. CI-630. PI-22 Informed That Conc. was 200M Out of TAOR. Reminded PI-22 That It Was a Registration Not a Conc. PI-22 Informed Me That a Registration Is Impossible Without Survey.

- 1620 - Requested Check Round on Conc. CI-217. Mortgage-3 Said That There Was No Reason To Fire Mission.

- 1830 - Sent In Night Position & On Call Illum. 27

<u>8 June 1965</u>

0745 - Requested Fire Mission At Coord 876078.
       Mortgage-3 Canceled Mission Saying Target Was Between
       Guns & FO.

0750 - Requested Fire Mission At Coord. 868075. Good
       Effect On Target. Conc CI-631.

1400 - Moved FO Team Away From Company Area
       And FAM Fired Our Weapons.

1830 - Sent In Night Position And On Call
       Illumination

<u>9 June 1965</u>

0810 - Requested Fire Mission At Coord. 866065
       Using HA For A Well Used Trail In The
       Draw Between Hill 106 & Hill 110. Excellent
       Effect On Target. Final Adjustment Was
       Right On Trail. Conc CI-632

0830 - Took Up New Daylight At 854075

1830 - Sent In Night Position And On Call Illum.

<u>10 June 1965</u>

1400 - Moved To Coord. 885087

1745 - Received Message From Mortage-3 To Move To
       Hill 144 For Security. There Was Something Of
       Intel. Nature That They Could Not Say Over Radio

                                                    28

1930 - REQU. 'TED TO FIRE CHECK ROUNDS ON CONCS.
IN OUR AREA, MORTGAGE-3 REFUSED.
1950 - SENT IN NIGHT POSITION & ON CALL ILLUM.

11 JUNE 1965

1700 - MOVED TO HILL 93 FOR NIGHT DEFENSE.

1715 - REQUESTED TO SHOOT A CONC. AT COORD. 865 088,
MORTGAGE-3 REFUSED.

1745 - SENT IN NIGHT POSITION & ON CALL ILLUMINATION.

1850 - PI-22 TOLD ME I COULD SHOOT ANY CONCS. I DEEMED
NECESSARY FOR NIGHT DEFENSE.

1855 - SENT PREVIOUSLY REQUESTED MISSION - CONC CI-636

1920 - ADJUSTED CHECK ROUNDS ON CONC. CI-401

1930 - ADJUSTED CHECK ROUNDS ON CONC. CI-904

1940 - ADJUSTED CHECK ROUNDS ON CONC. CI-811

12 JUNE 1965

0800 - REMAINED IN SAME POSITION USED SAME ON CALL ILLUM.

1840 - PI-4A RETURNED TO CP FOR PATROL WITH M-3 NEXT DAY

1850 - FIRED CONC CI-637

13 JUNE 1965

0800 - RETURNED TO BTRY AREA FOR DEBRIEFING BY
CAPT. HARMAN

29

DATE	EVENT

5 Jun 65   At 0630 three guns under Lt. Rosenberg returned to the area
            around Lang Xa village. Covering fires for a landing zone were
            fired while the helicopters were airborne using a restrictive
            fire plan. The battery fired 6 volleys using fuze VT and killed
            2 deer in the area. The helicopters landed with the smell of
            powder still in the air. The battery also fired prep fires on
            hill 303 for a blocking force which then swept the area using
            the hammer and anvil tactic. A number of huts and some
            equipment was destroyed but no VC were sighted.

6 Jun 65   Captain Harman went on liberty to Hue so the battery enjoyed a
            relaxing day. The switchboard operator noticed a considerable
            lapse in activity with Captain Harman's absence. The battery
            continued to fire H&I and on call missions.

30

DATE	ACTION

7-13 June   A conference was held at Hue to discuss the expansion of the TAOR and inparticular the A zone, which includes the Phu Bai complex. Among those in attendance were General Walt, Colonel Garretson, LtCol. Taylor and General Cheun, the Vietnamese 1st Division Commander. The result of this conference was that BLT 3/4 will have the responsibility for the "A" zone in the near future.

The Hue Phu Bai chapter of the international Playboy clubs was opened in the Battery "I" area on 12 June 1965. The bar was provided by 1stSgt "Hugh Hefner" Anderson and the decor is in the finest Battery "I" tradition, which is to say that the bar is decorated in contemporary playmate. Opening day festivities were also in the finest Battery "I" tradition.

Colonel Pala, 12th Marines Regemental CO visited the battery and inspected all the installations. His visit was completely unexpected and provided numerous constructive comments. The Colonel informed Captain Harman that in the future, critical supplies will be furnished by 1-12. Before he left the Colonel obtained a list of class 2 and class 5 requisitions which he will attempt to have filled from Okinawa.

The battery was alerted to possible large scale VC activity due in part to the change of government in Saigon. As a result of this danger, liberty in Hue has been cancelled until further notice.

Captain Harman was informed by Major Gibney via telephone that Lt. Bartels will become Hq Battery CO at Chu Lai. There is to be no Officer replacement for Lt. Bartels.

As of this date the battery has expended the following amounts of ammunition:

HE	WP	ILLUM	SMOKE	FZM500	VT
3,141	454	69	12	17	299

31

DATE   ACTION

7-13 June   Battery "I" had a close brush with disaster on Monday; the beer
            ration was cancelled. However, disaster was averted by the First
            Sergeant arranging with Captain Bao to procure beer through local
            sources. Even the First Sergeants efforts, however, were not
            enough to prevent the battery from going without beer for one
            entire day. Such a calamity will not be repeated as Captain
            Harman has directed that henceforth the battery will have beer
            every day.

            Also on Monday, the battery fired three concentrations using
            shell smoke into the area across the airfield near outpost 01,
            Phu-Bai. Captain Harman performed the duty of forward observer
            for this mission. The concentrations were only 900-1000 meters
            from the battery position so the battery personnel had the
            dubious privilege of listening to shells whistle close overhead.

            The next day Captain Harman and LtCol. Taylor reconoittered the
            Phu Bai village area and the colonel suggested that four
            concentrations be placed on the outskirts of the villages. Sgt
            McCardle will perform the survey of the area and within five
            days the battery will fire smoke into the area.

            Captain Harman also performed a reconaissance of the area around
            hill 303 at the request of the Colonel to see if the area would
            be suitable for artillery fire. The recon was done from a
            helicopter and the Captain saw signs of VC activity across the
            Ta Trach river which included a campfire, huts and a sanpan in
            the river. Since the area was out of range for Battery "I",
            Lt. Schaeffer arranged with Captain Bao to have the ARVN 155mm
            Howitzers fire a mission. Lt. Beery accompanied Captain Harman
            to adjust the fire. The campfire was put out by artillery fire
            since the VC were in too much of a hurry to do it themselves.

            As a result of this mission it was concluded that HE with fuze
            delay would be quite effective in the area so on Wednesday
            three guns were sent out to support an ambush set up by recon
            on the river. Sgt Taylor fired in 4 concentrations from hill
            225 to box in the ambush area. Sgt Taylor also used ARVN 155's
            to fire on 10 VC which were out of range of Battery "I". The
            battery stayed in position through the night with local security
            provided by an infantry platoon and fired H&I fires in the area
            of the ambush.

            On Thursday Lt Walker went up as an aerial observer and fired
            200 rounds on suspected VC positions. Intelligence dictates that
            two battalions of VC are located just outside the TAOR in this
            area. The battery fired H&I fires in the vicinity of this
            build up. Sgt Taylor used the ARVN 155's to fire on another
            10 VC's. Lt. Schaeffer went up in a helicopter to observe this
            mission. He estimated a possible 2 KIA's and also saw three
            sanpans in the river.

                                                                    61

DATE	ACTION

7-13 June   For the first time in over a week there was action on hill 180.
Lt. Broesamle, who replaced Lt. Soechtig on Wednesday spotted
almost 20 natives in white hats. The reaction force, accompanied
by Lt. Schacht was sent out to do battle but upon arriving at the
scene discovered that the "VC" were female and were too busy
picking berries to get involved in a fight. As harmless as they
seem, however, these berry-pickers have proved to be a great
headache to the battalion. Not only do they pick their berries
in our TAOR, but there is the ever-present possibility that the
baskets which are loaded with berries at the end of the day had
been loaded with mines and mortar rounds in the morning.

HMM 365 is due to depart on Saturday and units from HMM 161 have
been arriving to replace them. Lt. Townsend came with them to
pay a visit.

Cpl Little made a trip to Da Nang to scrounge (for want of a better
word) some bore cleaner and 8 in howitzer grid sheets. His trip,
however, was in vain. On a brighter side of supply, the battery
received 10 pairs of much needed boots.

Lt. Schacht and Lt. Walker have returned to the battery position
with their respective companies.

Priority of work has gone to the gun positions with concrete
slabs being poured and ammo pits being improved. The battery
is getting ready for the monsoon season. If the rains are as
bad as we have heard it may become necessary to save the ammo
boxes to build an ark.

TAD money was paid to the battery on Friday. Battery "I" was the
first unit to receive this pay as a result of many long hours of
work put in by Sgt Shanahan to prepare the orders.

A trig list has been prepared by Sgt McCardle. The battery has
yet to occupy a position that the guns haven't been laid by
orenting angle. The maps of the area are fairly accurate and the
FO's are familiar enough with them that initial rounds have been
within 100-200 meters of the target.

A band was provided, courtesy of Captain Bao, to entertain the
battery during Friday evening meal.

To date the battery has expended the following number of rounds

HE	WP	ILLUM	SMOKE	M500	VT
2618	454	69	12	17	299

62

DATE	ACTION

14 June   The battery made preparations for the visit of four members of
Congress; the Honorable Mssrs. Bray of Indiana, Pike of New York,
Gehard of Missouri, and Chamberlain of Michigan. Because of past
favorable impressions made by the Battery upon visiting dignitaries,
LtCol. Taylor directed that the S-3 charts be brought to the
battery position where the Colonel briefed the congressmen on the
TAOR. This was followed by a briefing by Capt. Harman on artillery
matters including Lt Beery's counter mortar board, and a briefing
by Corporal Rotella, section chief of gun #2 on the 105mm howitzer.
The visitors were duly impressed. Then the congressmen and their
constituents proceeded to the galley for cold drinks, coffee and
discussion. Unfortunately, the good impression was somewhat
lessened by the poor attitude of certain personnel from the BLT, and
particularly the tank platoon. Instead of sencere questions and
honest criticism, these individuals had what can only be described
as petty gripes which they aired in a definately rude manner. As
a result, other individuals who had important things to say, did not
have the opportunity to do so.

As a result of having assumed control of the "A" zone, the battery
is now laid in three different directions; Two guns on barrage data,
two down the center of the TAOR, and two on the Phu Bai village area
at the rear of the position. For this reason the battery operates a
battalion type FDC. Three permanent outposts, 180, 225 and 01 are
also occupied which causes personnel to be spread rather thin.

Enemy activity has increased in the past few days, but has all
occurred outside of the TAOR. Because of this situation an ambush
will be established by the recon platoon on the banks of the Ta
Trach river, near the edge of the TAOR Tuesday night.

15 June   Priority of work has gone to pouring cement and building up the gun
pits with crushed rock in preparation for the on coming rainy season.

Staff Sergeant Thomas reported to the battery, and was assigned the
post of battery gunnery sergeant. Gunnery Sergeant Satterfield will
replace Gunnery Sergeant ANDERSON, who is due to depart shortly, as
battery 1st Sgt. Staff Sergeant Thomas is a welcome addition to
the battery.

At 1700, three guns displaced 4,000 meters forward to support the
ambush which was established on the Ta Trach river by the recon
platoon. The ambush fired on a barge in the river and reported a
body floating in the water and a man, presumed wounded, crawling
up the opposite bank of the river. The body was not recovered.
Battery "I" fired illumination in support of the ambush and the
next morning fired 72 rounds for diversionary fire while the recon
platoon departed from the area.

32

DATE	ACTION
16 June	At 0800 the forward echelon of the battery returned to the position and concentrations were fired earlier in the morning.
17 June	Lt. Bartels departed the battery for Chu Lai where he will assume command of Headquarters Battery. He has served the battery long and well and his presence will be missed. Accompanying Lt. Bartels to Chu Lai were Sgt Pate, Cpl Baird and Pfc Jones. Sgt Pate went for a request mast with LtCol. Slack while Cpl Baird and Pfc Jones went to check on supply matters.

Capt. Harman attended a meeting at district headquarters to discuss the "A" zone. This "A" zone consists of three villages: Thuy Loung, Thuy Tan and Thuy Phu with populations of 4,800, 2,200 and 5,200 respectivly. The total population of the area is around 14,000 and if only 10% are VC sympathizers, this could be a problem area. Each village has a chief who are as follows: Thuy Luong – Phom Hy; Thuy Tan – Le dinh San; Thuy Phu – Le Kim Bat. In addition, each village is subdivided into hamlets, a single village having as many as five hamlets.

Lt. Miller, the Supply Officer for 1/12 visited the battery to discuss supply problems.

Gunnery Sergeant Satterfield visited three hamlets in the Laotion area in order to inspect gun positions there. These were the hamlets of Tabat, Ahshan and Tuy Le. Lt. Weld went with Capt. Bao to visit the tomb of Minh Manh. There were no gun positions in the tomb but he took the Captains camera so the purpose of the "recon" can be surmised.

| 18 June | During the morning the battery fired smoke on four concentrations in the area around Phu Bai village. Capt. Bao, Capt. Young and LtCol Taylor observed the firing of these missions. LCpl Lamb fired a mission from 225 on three VC. Two KIA's were confired as a result of this mission. |

During the afternoon the battalion commanders inspection was held with good results.

| 19 June | First Sergeant Anderson, Sergeant Boise and Sergeant Thompkins departed from the battery on normal rotation. These men have been valuable to the battery and will be missed. |

The priority of work is still with the gun pits and the battery continues to haul crushed rock to build up the positions for the rainy season.

33

DATE	ACTION

19 June   Major Ruthazer, 3/4 S-3, toured the battery area and inspected the defenses.

"K" Company participated in a joint operation with the Panther Company of the ARVN. The Panther Company is composed of men who have had kinfolks murdered by the Viet Cong. They are distinguished by a solid red scarf worn around the neck and are among the most dedicated of the ARVN forces for obvious reasons. The operation was a hammer and anvil type sweep conducted along the Ta Trach river to Joilette. The ARVN had considerable activity, killing 22 VC, but "K" Company, operating on the opposite bank, had no activity at all.

LCpl Lamb on hill 225 fired on a VC campfire at the base of hill 303. He succeeded in puting the fire out.

I Corps intelligence suspected a VC OP to be located about 4,000m from the Phu Bai village complex. Lt. Walker adjusted a mission on the suspected OP and succeeded in flushing out four VC. The reactionary force was sent out but the VC fled into the village.

34

Date	Action
20 June	

One section of the battery displaced forward to fire on the reverse slope of hill 303. Lt. Beery and S/Sgt Thomas accompanied the forward echelon and fired eight observed missions into suspected VC bivouac areas. The battery also fired 120 unobserved rounds because intelligence indicated two VC battalions in the area. For this reason the battery will continue to displace guns forward to within artillery range of these areas. Concurrently with these missions, Lt. Schacht and GySgt Satterfield fired on hill 225 with the remainder of the battery. Major Watson, Captain Harman and Cpl Marlatt went to hill 225 to observe the firing there. Lt Cross was the FO. The purpose of firing on 225 was to register close in defensive concentrations, and because of the excellent shooting, some of these concentrations were as close as 50 meters. This use of artillery would make it very difficult to capture hill 225. This ability to shoot and displace the battery by section and occupy two positions simultaneously is a credit to the whole battery as it is the mark of good artillery.

General Karch toured the battery area and inspected each individual gun pit. He informed the battery CO that this is the best laid out battery with the best gun pits he has seen in Viet Nam. This is especially encouraging coming from an artilleryman.

Officers and Staff NCO's are filling billets as follows:

Lt. Beery - XO
Lt. ROSENBERG - FDO
Lt. SCHAEFFER - LnO
Lt. SCHACHT - Asst XO
Lt. WALKER - FO "I" Co
Lt. CROSS - FO "L" Co
Lt. WELD - FO "K" Co
Lt. HENDERSON - FO "M" Co
Lt. SOECHTIG - NGF Spotter
Lt. BROESAMLE - NGF LnO
GySgt SAFFERFIELD - 1stSgt
SSgt THOMAS - GySgt
SSgt HODGE - Operations Chief
SSgt MCKISSICK - Comm Chief

35

DATE	ACTION

21 June   Liberty in Hue for the battery was resumed after a lapse of
twelve days, and the improvement of the battery position
continues as usual.

General Throckmorton and General Walt were scheduled to visit
3/4 and again Battery "I" was chosen as the vantage point
LtCol. Taylor was to have the S-3 charts set up behind gun #2
and give a briefing on the TACR followed by Capt. Harman whose
subject was artillery defensive fire plans and the counter
mortar board. However, General Throckmorton did not show up
and after a short briefing General Walt called the battery
and attachments together for a speech. A barrel was provided
for him to stand on but he declined using it because he said
he would probably fall off and break his neck. The General said
that artillery, infantry and naval gunfire are all necessary to
a successful war effort and it would be impossible to say which
was most important. He linked them to a football team because
the team can't function properly without all of its members.
He then went on to give examples of the effectiveness of artillery.
He told how at Chu Lai an ARVN platoon was attacked by a VC
battalion and threatened with annihilation. The platoon called
for artillery support from an 8 inch platoon. The platoon fired
40 rounds, chasing the VC 1200 yards while killing 85 and wounding
65. In his own career the general told how his life was saved
by artillery when the Japanese made a banzi attack during WW II.
The artillery fired within 50m of the friendly position killing
300 out of 500 of the attacking force. The general also said
that the MAF is the best fighting force ever assembled and that
Battery "I" has the best reputation of any artillery unit in
Viet Nam. He said that in this war every man must know his
job and that he had heard nothing but compliments about this
battery. Concerning the future the general said he expects this
to be a long war. He does not expect much action until the
monsoon season. However, when the rains begin the VC will
become active. At this time he said, we will not even be able
to see the tops of the mountains and air support will often be
impossible. It will be up to the FO's and the artillery to
provide support. He advised digging in and getting prepared.
The general closed by saying it will be necessary to be able
to drop shells within 100m of friendly lines. The troops were
impressed by the general and his speech.

36

DATE	ACTION
21 June (Cont)	"K" Company inaugerated the people to people program in the "A" Zone by going into Thuy Phu village. The purpose was to give the people a chance to see the Marines in person and the Marines built up good will by distributing candy to the children, shopping in the local markets etc.. This program shows promise of being quite successful.

Capt. Harman went with Sgt McCardle and the survey team into the area and picked out likely routes of approach such as bridges etc. for survey. This type of reconnaissance is another purpose of the people to people program.

| 22 June | "I" Company continued the people to people program by making a visit to Thuy Tan village. The visit got off to a spectacular start when the bumper of a truck caught the arch which marked the entrance of the village and pulled it down. Fortunately there weren't two many spectators (perhaps witnesses would be a better word) and the incident was soon forgotten. Other than that the visit was a complete success. |

Three guns from the battery were ordered to displace forward with 600 rounds of ammunition in order to fire on 2 suspected battalions of VC outside the TAOR toward Laos. Lt. Walker acted as AO using an army OE observation aircraft which was furnished through liaison with I Corps. Lt. Walker fired three missions on suspected supply areas and positions. He also performed aerial reconnaissance of the area where the two battalions were supposed to be but had negative results. The three guns remained in position throughout the night with security provided by "K" Company. Lt. Beery acted as FDO for the forward echelon while Lt. Schacht held the position of Executive Officer. Lt. Rosenberg and Lt. Cross remained with the rear echelon as FDO and Executive Officer respectivly.

Lt. Broesamle replaced Lt. Soechtig on hill 180. Additional fortification of that OP has been in progress because of the possibility that a battalion of VC may attempt to capture one of the permanent OP's for propaganda reasons.

| 23 June | The rear echelon of the battery fired H&I fires during the night to confuse the enemy while the forward echelon fired 80 rounds of unobserved fire on the reverse side of hill 303. At about 0800 Lt. Schacht, in his capacity of Exec for the forward echelon, returned the three guns to the battery position. |

37

DATE	ACTION

23 June
(Cont)

Work continues to improve the battery position with the current project being to rebuild the ammunition stowage areas.

Lt. Weld has assumed the duties of mess officer. Work is in progress to pour a cement deck for the galley and continued until 0300 by candlelight under the watchful eye of Lt. Weld.

Capt. Harman and Capt. Dao discussed the concentrations which will be plotted in Thuy Phu.

24 June

After two evenings of working under candlelight the cement deck in the galley has been completed.

Lt. Henderson, "H" Company FO, spotted 10 VC, and his company received sniper fire. The reaction force was sent out but the VC escaped before the force could arrive, one Marine from "H" Company stepped on a land mine and the explosion killed him and another Marine while wounding an additional two. Lt. Henderson is investigating this incident.

A suspected VC outpost was fired on from hill 225 during the afternoon.

H&I fires continued throughout the night.

Intelligence indicates that there is a build-up of VC in the southern portion of the TAOR. The area is out of range of the 105mm howitzers so it would be necessary for the battery to displace in order to take targets there under fire. It has been recommended that the morning recon flights include an FO in the left seat of the helecopter.

Preparations have been made to fire smoke in the Thuy Phu areas on Saturday. The district chief as well as the village chiefs and LtCol. Taylor will observe this mission.

25 June

LCpl Baird with PFC Jones and PFC Sharp went to Chu Lai to pick up supply equipment. Among the equipment was an embrossing machine which will make the heavy workload of Sgt Shanahan and PFC Woodhouse a little lighter.

The battery continues to fire H&I fires and is scheduled to displace 3 times next week in order to fire on suspected enemy positions near the Loation border.

38

DATE	ACTION

25 June
(Cont)

At the present time only one line company and the recon platoon are patrolling the TAOR. The other three Companies are involved in local security and strengthining the perimeter as well as providing a quick reaction force. The use of an extra line company for local security has allowed Battery "I" to relinquish two of its outposts. In addition, OP 01 has been moved to the control tower in the airfield. These measures have been taken in preparation for the monsoon season.

The assistant Commandant of the Royal Thai Navy paid a visit to 3/4 and toured the battery area with Lt. Beery.

Captain Harman submitted a letter to LtCol. Taylor concerning the use of FO's as aerial observers on helecopter recon flights. This was prompted by intelligence reports of the possibility of a build-up of VC strength near hill 303. The recommendation was accepted and as a result, Lt. Walker and Lt. Cross will occupy the left seat on the helecopters as AO's during these flights.

Improved fortifications continue to be constructed on hill 180 and hill 225.

Liberty in Hue now goes on odd days for BLT 3/4 with 8th MTU and Hd.-161 being granted liberty on the even days.

26 June

Cpl. Baird departed the battery as a member of the July draft. He has served the battery well as supply NCO and his presence will be missed.

Captain Harman conferred with the village chiefs of Thuy Tan, Thuy Phu and Thuy Luong. Survey was accomplished in the Phu Bai village area for four concentrations which were located on the narrow strip between route #1 and the railroad. These concentrations were then fired using shell smoke. The Regimental Executive Officer, LtCol. Brooks, LtCol. Taylor, the village chiefs and numerous villagers witnessed the firing of these missions. PFC Catoe acted as FC while Capt. Harman explained the proceedings. All rounds landed within 20m of the targets, one of them even knocking down the red flag designating the target. Everyone was duly impressed and the credit must go to the entire battery; notably survey FDC, the guns with a little credit reserved for lady luck. After

DATE	ACTION

26 June
(Cont)

this impressive demonstration, the village chiefs desire many more concentrations in the area. This will require a great deal of difficult survey involving triangulation because of the lack of trig points.

Capt. Harman, Lt. Beery, and LCpl Huss attended a farewell party for Capt. Young, USA, at 8th RRU. The party was a festive affair including Vietnamese entertainment and a seven course dinner.

The battery maintains its excellent relationship with the 12th ARVN Artillery. On three occasions during this week alone, the ARVN fired missions for Battery "I" which were out of range for the 105mm howitzer and six reinforcing missions.

DATE	ACTION

28 June   Lt. Statler joined the battery today. He will go to hill 225 to build an OP bunker and man the O.P.

Sgt McCardle accompanied an ARVN survey team to Thuy Luong and Thuy Tan. It is expected that survey will be completed in these areas and the battery can fire the concentrations with shell smoke on Saturday.

The battery fired prep fires for an ARVN exercise which were coordinated by Capts. MacKenzie and MacDonald, Australian advisiors at Dang Da. Lt Weld did the adjusting. The fires were quite impressive and could be seen from the battery area.

The BLT Commander desires to start fires in the jungle during the dry season. To accomplish this the battery fired 6 battery 6's in the area which succeeded in starting a number of fires.

29 June   Action began early when Lt. Walker accompanied the recon platoon in a penetration of the jungle. The platoon got off the helecopters and penetrated about 100m into the jungle when automatic weapons fire broke out from three spots followed by mortar incoming on the landing zone. The recon platoon commander decided on immediate evacuation from the area. Before leaving 1 VC who stepped out onto the trail was killed. Another VC who attempted to retrieve the body was shot at and possibly wounded. However, the evacuation by recon did not end the affair. Two men were mistakenly left behind so the reaction force was sent out to pick them up. unfortunatly the reactionary force then left behind one of its own men and had to return again to pick him up. Lt. Walker and Cpl Marlatt accompanied this force.

Later in the morning Lt. Walker made a flight in an OE as an aerial observer and fired in the same area. Still later he accompanied the FAC to point out terrain features for an air strike.

At about 0900, the battery sent out three guns to the Oasis in support of the recon operation. The other three were to have followed at 1500 but did not do so because the operation was later cancelled. The three forward guns spotted nine VC on a ridge line 2,000 meters away and fired 5 rounds in direct fire which sent the VC in hasty retreat. The forward guns also fired for Lt. Walker, as AO and for 225 as well as numerous other missions in the jungle area. In all 272 rounds were expended. Lt. Beery was in command of the forward echelon while Lt. Schacht remained with the rear. The forward echelon returned at about 1800.

41

DATE	ACTION

1 July

Battery "I" made preparations to support a sweep of the jungle area south of hill 303 by "L" Company. 200 rounds of diversionary fires were fired by series from 0430 to 0530. At 0530 a forward echelon of three guns displaced to the Oasis. Lt. Beery and SSgt Thomas accompanied the forward echelon while Lt. Schacht and GySgt Satterfield remained with the rear. At 0630 "L" Company was helelifted into the landing zone which had been prepared by the rear 3 guns using fuze VT. Lt. Walker was on station in an L-19 and fired on suspected harboring sights and possible VC positions forward of the sweep. Lt. Cross with "L" Company fired 3 observed missions also. At 1300 the company came out of the jungle. No VC had been sighted but there was considerable evidence as to their presence.

Lt. Beery had with his three guns: 2 tanks, 3 ontos and a rifle platoon. He used the two tanks and the three howitzers to make a five gun battery. Lt. Beery laid the tanks and with SSgt Hodge using tank gunnery, Lt. Statler adjusted indirect fire with the five gun battery from hill 225 a range of 9000m. Amazingly the tanks and artillery rounds held together. Equally amazing was the performance of the Ontos. Lt. Beery used Ontos gunnery and Lt. Statler adjusted indirect fire for them, obtaining accuracy within 50m at a range of 8000m. However, the afternoon ended on an unfortunate note when a premature burst from a superquick round exploded 26m from gun 6 injuring two men. Pfc Becker was not seriously injured but the other man, Cpl Bartelt required surgery to remove a fragment from his chest. Fortunately he will recover and return to duty in about 30 days.

2 Companies of VC were spotted by ARVN in Thuy Toung and Thuy Tain. A successful sweep was conducted resulting in 73 KIA's and the capture of 2 60mm mortars. The battery supported this operation, knocking out a bunker and firing illumination. The action took place in the northern portion of the TAOR.

2 July

At about 0620, Lt. Cross with "L" Company made contact with 5 VC while making a sweep of the area west of 225. "L" Company had one man wounded by sniper fire before losing contact with the VC. LCpl Boehme, also with "L" Company, was fired at by helecopters of HMM-161 at about 1300. 161 reported that they were firing at a target across the river and the gunner got carried away.

Lt. Soechtig with Cpl Marlatt went out during the afternoon as an FO Team for a recon squad. They patrolled the eastern edge of the TAOR from Phuoe Tam to hill 28. On hill 28, the recon squad planned a defensive position while Lt. Soechtig called in a defensive concentration. This will be used in the future when recon sets up a squad defense on hill 28. Shell smoke had to be used because of civilians in the area, and the concentration was within 200m of the position.

42

DATE	ACTION

2 July (Cont)

Cpl Little went out with another squad from recon as an FO. This squad patrolled an area to the east of hill 225 on a route extending generally north to south. Cpl Little shot in defensive concentrations for future recon ambushes on hills 106, 116 and several routes of approach.

Lt. Walker went as an AO to investigate a report of 1000 VC at the southwestern edge of the TAOR. However, he did not see any signs of the enemy in the area.

During the night both battery "I" and 12th ARVN fired H&I fires into those areas where VC had been reported during the day.

3 July

General Krulak paid another visit to BLT 3/4. As far as Battery "I" was concerned, there were a couple of interesting highlights to this trip. The first was when the general and Lt.Col. Taylor paid a visit to hill 225 where Lt. Henderson was awaiting them. For demonstration purposes, Lt. Henderson fired concentration CI 958 which would have been quite impressive had the round gone off which it didn't. Lt.Col. Taylor thought the round probably went into the jungle but General Krulak, not jumping to hasty conclusions, asked Lt. Henderson where he thought it had gone. Lt. Henderson, using cool logic replied that either the round was a dud or there had been a large change in the met message. The general seemed satisfied.

Also on the agenda was a trip to Phu Bai village for a demonstration of the concentrations there using shell smoke. Accompanying the general were Capt. Harman and Sgt. McCardle. The village chief, Le Kim Bat, using a homemade map, called in the concentration which was appropriately designated concentration Bat. The round hit right on target, but more impressive to the general was the village chief's ability to call in the fire. General Krulak autographed the chiefs map at his request as a gesture of admeration. The general also requested Capt. Harman to submit a written report outlining the plan for use of artillery in the Phu Bai village area.

4 July

It was a quiet Independence day, the only military activity being check rounds fired by Cpl Little who was patrolling with recon.

An American Flag was flown over the battery position and many troops took this opportunity to take pictures as it was the first time the flag has been flown in a long time. After dark illumination was fired at 360° around the TAOR which made a suitable substitute for the traditional fireworks.

5 July

Sgt McCardle went to Phu Bai to continue the survey which is necessary for the concentrations there. Because of increasing danger in the area, he is no longer permitted to travel alone and took an infantry squad along for security. Meanwhile Capt. Harman showed Capt. Rickleck, "M" Company Commander, the battery defenses because "M" Company will be staying in the battery area for awhile. 43

DATE	ACTION

5 July
(Cont)

The L-19 observation aircraft arrived. Coordination was quickly achieved and it was established that the battery would furnish AO's on ten minutes notice when necessary. Lt's Walker and Henderson took the first flights and fired WP on hill 153 in order to start fires, with good results. Observation flights to check the TAOR and to search for and fire upon enemy targets will be conducted daily.

Col. Wheeler and Mr. Duncan, correspondant for the New York Times visited BLT 3/4, and were briefed by Capt. Harman in the FDC tent. The briefing was also attended by the Captains pet goat who showed up unexpectedly and unenvited. However, he proved an attentive spectator having found a confortable position behind the switchboard.

The long awaited shower unit has been completed and is located near the FDC tent. An ice machine capable of producing 1500 lbs of ice a day is expected in the near future. These two items will make living conditions in the battery area considerably more comfortable.

The July draft finally departed. Included in this group were Cpl Dunson and LCpl's Cannon, Newbill and Smith.

Lt. Soechtig and Cpl Marlatt who are in the field with "K" Company fired a mission on a suspected VC OP.

6 July

Improvement of the battery position continued with the strong-backing of a third tent in the galley area being completed. This was the Officer/Staff mess tent which will also be supplied with tables and chairs paid for by the Officers/Staff and Sgt's concerned.

Captain Harman and Sgt McCardle conducted a recon of the forward area near the tin shack in the vicinity of hill 180 in order to select possible new battery positions. Lt. Henderson accompanied by Lt. Tim (ARVN) as interpreter, proceeded to Thuy Loung to establish survey for additional concentrations.

The battery fired on a defilade area of hill 36 with good results. H&I fires continue in heavy volume although there has been very little reported enemy activity in the TAOR.

LtCol. Taylor informed the battery that it is under the administrative control of 1/12. Therefore, all personnel replacements and promotions will be handled by 1/12. However, 3/12 still controls logistics and supply matters. This arrangement was established by division and could create some difficulties for the battery because it will be necessary to "serve two masters".

44

DATE	ACTION

— 7 July   Capt. Harman and Sgt Shanahan went to Da Nang to coordinate with 1/12 concerning the administrative matters mentioned on 6 July.

The battery moved three guns under the command of Lts. Beery and Schacht to the tin shack area which had been reconned earlier by Capt. Harman. The displacement was made to support a hammer and anvil sweep by "K" Company in the jungle, below 303. "K" Company remained in the jungle until 1430 but had no VC contact and did not use artillery preparation because it might warn any VC in the area of the operation. However, Lt. Henderson acting as AO in an L-19 fired missions west of "K" Companies area. Lt. Rosenberg remained with the rear echelon and the forward echelon returned at 1430 when "K" Company left the jungle.

LtCol. Taylor and Capt. Harman had a meeting to discuss the moving of 6 81mm mortars to the battery position. They also discussed the completing of the concentrations at Thuy Phu, Thuy Luong and Thuy Tam and the firing of these concentrations. The Colonel mentioned that there is the possibility of an attack on the 20th of July and that we should be especially alert at this time.

Lt. Statler continues improvement of the position on hill 225 and requested materials to be sent for this purpose.

— 8 July   An AO schedual has been established for the L-19's.

As a result of yesterday's meeting, 6 81mm mortars will be attached to the battery and will be placed on the east flank of the position with the primary sector of fire being the airfield. The battery CO, will have operational but not administrative responsibility for the mortars.

Lt. Henderson and Sgt McCardle completed the survey to Thuy Tam.

GySgt Satterfield made a trip to Da Nang to effect liaision with 1/12 while Pfc's Jones and Woodhouse went to Chu Lai on Supply Matters.

Capt. Harman made liaision with Capt. Bao and Capt Taylor concerning the upcoming Marine/ARVN combined operation. Artillery aspects of the operation were discussed and the mission of the battery will be to provide direct support to 3/4 and reinforcement to ARVN. A CPX will be held prior to the operation as a form of rehersal.

Three guns again displaced to the tin shack area to fire for Lt. Henderson who was acting as AO in an L-19. They fired with good effect in the defilade area around 303.

45

DATE	ACTION

8 July
(Cont)

Intelligence data extracted from infrared photos indicate 4 VC battalions massing outside of the TAOR.

Letters of Commendation for Lt. Weld and GySgt Satterfield were submitted to battalion.

LCpl's Pierce and Lamb returned from a three day R&R trip to Saigon making a total of four men that the battery has sent so far.

Lt. Soechtig, FO with "K" Company, fired WP on an area where VC snipers have been previously sighted in preparation for patrols around hill 143 tomorrow.

9 July

Capt. Harman with Lt. Henderson and Sgt McCardle went to Thuy Loung to fire in concentrations for the village Chief Phan Hy. The concentrations fired were Thi, Hy, Ngot, Chan and Hg, being named after noble villagers rather than designated by numbers. Survey data proved to be excellent and the concentrations were adjusted by Capt. Harman. The only problem encountered was in keeping the Marine recon squad and the villagers out of the impact area. Phan Hy was pleased with the concentrations and brought the party back to his headquarters for beer. At 0930 the party proceeded to Thuy Tan where concentrations Senh and Tren were fired for the village chief Le Dinh Sad. These were adjusted by Capt. Harman to within 100m of the party, a feat which testifies to the skill and accuracy of the survey, FDC and gun crews.

General Karch visited 3/4 and was briefed by Lt. Beery on the charts and the counter-mortar board. LCpl Potter briefed him on the guns and the general remarked that Potter was on of the sharpest LCpl's he had seen. The general also informed the battery that a battery of 155mm howitzers and a battery of howtars would be coming to Phu Bai with a Hq Battery to form an artillery group. The general also went to Thuy Tam to observe the effects of the artillery "people to people" program. The concentration that Capt. Harman had fired there earlier was fired for his benefit.

12th ARVN artillery and Battery "I" fired mutual reinforcing fires on hill 153 with Capt. Bao and Capt. Harman acting as FO's. It may be a little unusual for a battery and a battalion commander to act as FO's but the effect was excellent with both units massing fires on the target.

10 July

At 0530 3 guns displaced to the Lang Xa area to support the combined Marine and ARVN operation in the An Ninh area. Two Ontos preceeded the battery to the position and one of them hit an AT mine which destroyed the right suspension system. The battery remained in the Lang Xa position until 1500. Details of this operation are in the attached enclosure.

46

BRIEF ON BATTERY "I" SUPPORT OF ARVN OPERATIONS IN
VICINITY OF AN NINH (9-11 JULY 1965)

P.I. 22 B and radio operator (Lt. Cross and LCpl Johnson) moved with
Mortgage 3 and party to Hue for final coordination conference of Advisors and
their ARVN counterparts on the afternoon of the ninth. Lt. Cross acted as
artillery liaison officer for the USMC as Battery "I" was to be used in the following operation as reinforcing fires for ARVN artillery (4) 105mm Howitzers
and (2) 155mm Howitzers being employed in the operation.

The ARVN were attempting to maintain great secrecy of this operation by
holding apparent last minute briefings at locations quite distant from the
actual operating area to be used also intensive H&I fires had been fired the
previous night at P.K. 17 (17 Kil north of Hue) in hopes that the V.C. would
think that the operation was to be conducted in the north (the vicinity of
many recent ARVN operations). At 0600 the following morning the command group
of the 3rd ARVN Regt., 1st Division moved to the area of the Regt. C.P. for this
operation at An Ninh. Command group included Regt. Officers staff and Advisors
and Liaison group from BLT 3/4 including myself (Lt. Cross) as Marine Artillery
liaison and Mortgage 3 (Maj. Ruthazer) as BLT liaison. At this time a 16 plane
Marine and Navy air strike commenced preparing both landing zones to be used
and probable V.C. locations. Simultaneously the elite Black Panther Company
and an APC Company moved thru us and prepared to cross the river from the
north and move into the objective area. Black Panther Company is a very
interesting unit both in dress and personnel as they dress with black berets
and jungle utilities, and are the best trained of the 1st Division ARVN units.
They are used whenever a quick moving highly effective strike force is needed.

By the time the Battery had displaced to its forward position and as the
air strike ended the Huey gun-ships moved in to the area to support and protect
the air lift of the first and third ARVN battalion. The actual regimental C.P.
at this time was airborne in a Huey slick and would not be at our position
until the troop lifts were completed and ground forces organized.

As soon as the ARVN forces were landed, aft of Marine forces "K", M(-), and
I(-), would be accomplished placing their blocking positions on the other side
of the river. The ARVN would attempt to push any V.C. in the area in their
sweeping operations to the river (Song Tra Trach) where they could either be
eliminated by Marine infantry across the river or by the ARVN. While the 1st
and 3rd Battalions were accomplishing this sweep the Black Panther Company and
APC Company would quickly sweep down from the north and both block from the
north and thoroughly cover the area of the tomb of Gia Long (This is a very
extensive almost 2 grid squares) tomb complex of the first king of Viet Nam.
The complex includes the tombs of his wife and mother and had been the scene
of much V.C. activity the week before. A V.C. force estimated at 2 Companies
had surrounded a ARVN regional Company and inflicted some casulties until
Marine choppers had come into the area.

41

As the day progressed the ARVN forces smoothly took their assigned objectives with no contacts occuring until 1200 when in the apace of an hour they killed (8) V.C. and captured (4) weapons. These V.C. were scattered groups that were attempting to hide their weapons and get out of the area. Another V.C. was captured, slightly wounded, a short time later when ARVN engineer boats checking the river banks spotted him hiding in the water. The Black Panther Company had no contact around the tomb area although finding many signs of very recent V.C. occupancy.

Around 1430, ARVN secured their final objectives and the Marine blocking forces began to displace by air. "K" company and the Battery both displaced at 1530.

Around 1300 we were informed that because of the speed of completion of Phase I, that Phase II would be moved up one day and would commense early the following day.

P.I. 22 B (Lt. Cross) had no means of secure communications with P.I. 22 so had to inform the battery by most expeditous means possible. Mortgage 3 who was returning to Phu Bai area since the Marine units had displaced and were now out of the operation. Since neither battery were committed to a preparation at the beginning of Phase II this change in schedule had to be given to them.

The Black Panther Company and APC Company moved out of the objective area and Tornado Company moved in position as Regt. C.P. Security,

At 1930 received call that P.I. would not be able to fire the preparation.

Communicated this information to ARVN Regt. CO and the senior adviser and immediate arrangements were made to bring in (2) more 105's from Phu Bai area and to shift the prepatory fires to cover the whole area.

The reason that the Battalion was not able to displace was that since an Ontos acting as security for the Battery had hit a mine that day, Mortgage 6 (Col. Taylor) would not allow us to displace without prior road clearance.

Following morning Phase II commenced with 12 plane Phantom air strike on the objective area behind hill 419. This was followed by intensive WP preparation by ARVN artillery. They fired in all 550 105 rds and 80 155 rounds in the space of 35 minutes. ARVN forces moving to the line of departure killed (4) more V.C. and captured (1) weapon.

After the preparation was fired we received word that the Battery would not be displacing at all and I therefore made arrangements for my return to the BLT area.

GEORGE R. CROSS
1stLt.   USMC

48

59

DATE	ACTION

10 July
(Cont)

Major Beaty and Capt. Patterson visited the battery and informed the CO, of the formation of the artillery groupment, mentioned by General Karch, Major Beaty will be the groupment CO and a task organization is forthcoming. The Major inspected the inner defense area and selected proposed sites for the 155 battery, the howtar battery and the artillery Hq.

11 July

Major Beaty and Capt. Patterson toured the TAOR by helecopter with Capt. Harman, stopping at hills 225 and 180. On 225 Lt. Statler has been making good progress in constructing an artillery bunker there while Lt. Broesamle has kept everything squared away on 180.

LtCol. Taylor held a conference with Major Beaty and Capt. Harman during which the positions for the forthcoming artillery units were decided upon.

Major Beaty, Capt. Patterson, Capt. Harman and LCpl Huss toured the "A" zone by vehicle visiting Thuy Phu, Thuy Tan and Thuy Luong. From there the party went to Hue to inspect the point at which the artillery will debark. Capt. Harman spent the night in Hue with Major Watson at the american consulate. Major Watson is leaving to be releived by Major Zimmerman as Battalion Executive Officer.

The battery received two staff sergeants and two sergeants from 1/12. They are SSgt Brewer, SSgt Hollier, Sgt Tullar and Sgt Cylar. SSgt Brewer will become battery Gunnery Sergeant and SSgt Hollier will be the Motor Transport Chief while Sgt's Tullar and Cylar will become section chiefs. They are a welcome addition to the battery.

49

DATE	ACTION

12 July   Major Beaty and Capt. Patterson departed the battery for Da Nang.

The area had its first rainy day in quite some time and it rained quite hard until about 1400. This was a much needed storm as it washed down the tents and generally cooled off the whole area.

Lt. Soechtig returned from the field with "K" Company while Lt. Walker departed with "I" Company.

The battery continues to fire check rounds and H&I fires but there have been few observed missions lately.

13 July   Lt. Statler returned from hill 225 to be replaced by Lt. Weld while Lt. Broesmale came down from hill 180 after three weeks (a new record for Officers) having been replaced by Lt. Henderson.

Three guns displaced to the tin shack to support a sweep by "I" Company in the hill 153 area. "I" Company was reinforced by two platoons of "K" Company for this operation. The first platoon of "K" Company flushed three VC and in a running fight (the VC did most of the running and the platoon did the fighting) killed one of the VC. The battery did not have an opportunity to fire because the VC mentioned was the only contact made.

The priority of work has gone to engineering tasks such as strong-backing etc. An inspection routine has also been established as follows: Headquarters platoon on Monday, Firing Platoon on Tuesday and 81mm Mortars on Wednesday. Inspections will be functional rather than formal and are designed only to insure that all personnel have sufficient clothing and equipment and that it is in servicable condition.

14 July   A party consisting of Capt. Harman, Lt. Dau, 12th ARVN artillery. Le Kim Bat, Sgt McCardle and a squad from "I" Company went to the Phu Bai complex to fire in more smoke concentrations. After the shooting, tea was served and the party had an opportunity to sample the well known bettle nut which by all reports was abominable. Capt. Harman also had a long conversation with Le Kim Bat during which he learned that the village chief had served nine years with the French Army and is a VC killer from way back. One of the chief's ambitions is to take a helecopter ride and if this can be arranged he promised to tell the captain when the VC are in the village so the battery rather than the popular force can shoot them. There were, he said, 7 VC in the village two nights ago. The chief keeps an autographed picture of General Krulak on his desk next to a smoke round which he also has as a souveneir. Capt. Harman was offered a dog for a pet but this was graceously though firimly declined.

50

DATE	ACTION

14 July (Cont)

Lt. Walker reported seeing approximately 70 VC just outside the TAOR and this was confirmed by Lt. Weld from hill 225. Lt. Beery then reconned the area in an L-19 and reported that the individuals were civilians rather than VC. Intelligence sources informed that these were refugees that had been expelled from their village by the VC.

Lt. Weld spotted 3 VC swimming in a pond near the base of 225. Since they were within 106mm recoiless rifle and 50 cal Machine Gun range, the artillery was used to cut off their route of retreat while the 106's fired on the pond. A direct hit was scored but no bodies were recovered. It is suspected that they are on the bottom of the pond and should come floating up any day now.

General Walt and Col. Wheeler had lunch in the battery area after the general gave a talk to the men of "M" Company. It was the same sort of talk he gave to the battery about a month ago.

A doctor of Bethesda Naval Hospital has been in the area checking the malaria conditions. He spent a night on 225 being bitten by, and collecting mosquitoes. (The troops on 225 just get bitten; they don't collect them but that is because they are not involved in research). This area apparently has one of the highest malaria rates in Viet Nam.

15 July

This was a day of very little activity two culverts, using 55 gallon drums with the ends removed, were placed in position across the battery road.

16 July

Intelligence dictates a possible buildup of VC to the rear of hill 303. Accordingly, LtCol. Taylor directed that three guns move forward to the Khe Cam Thu river to deal with this threat. At the same time Lt. Beery functioned as AO in an L-19. A patrol from recon spotted five individuals who appeared to be digging holes, but the artillery was not permitted to fire presumably because the nature of the target was not exactly known. Instead the recon patrol went to investigate, but failed to make contact. Lt. Beery spotted about 50 civilians on the southern side of hill 303 and the BLT CO decided that we should shoot at them because it was possible they were bringing supplies to the VC. Accordingly the battery fired zone fire which was adjusted by Lt. Beery. The battery also fired on a suspected hospital, and OP and a small group of huts all of which were located on the edge of the jungle. In all, about 100 rounds were expended and the battery returned to base camp at about 1100.

51

DATE	ACTION

16 July (Cont)

Capt. Patterson arrived with the recon party from 4/12. The battalion is due to begin coming in by air starting at about 1000 on the 17th of July. The artillery group will consist of the Hq Battery 4/12, CMR 4/12, Howtar Battery 2/12 and "M" Battery 4/12. The Howtar Battery will be the first to arrive. "M" Battery is a 155mm towed howitzer battery instead of the self-propelled howitzers which were originally expected. The task organization for this group is still forthcomming. Sgt McCardle is already conducting the survey for the group while SSgt McKissick is laying the wire.

Sgt Shanahan and Sgt McCardle went to Da Nang to visit 1/12 on administrative matters. Battery "I" now comes under the administrative control of 4/12. In three months the battery has come under the control of 3/12, division, 1/12 and now 4/12. This averages out to a change every three weeks which should constitute some sort of record.

Shortly after dark, "I" Company had a grenade thrown into their night ambush position. Lt. Walker called for illumination which was denied, but was given permission to fire WP. He fired 3 rds of WP and again requested illumination. His request was granted, but low burst illumination had to be used. Two rounds were fired with negative results.

17 July

Large numbers of civilians continue to frequent the TAOR. Lt. Weld observed about 35 from hill 225 and fired HE in their vicinity. However, the HE did not frighten them as expected so a smoke round was fired into their midst. This succeeded in convincing them to leave the area.

Lt. Statler with Cpl Marlatt as his radio operator accompanied a recon patrol into the "A" Zone.

Lt. Schacht replaced Lt. Henderson on hill 180 and will remain there for a few days.

The Officers and Staff NCO mess has been greatly improved by the addition of 8 new tables.

4/12 began arriving with the C-134's bringing in 86 chock loads of equipment. Howtars arrived first to be followed by "M", Hq and CMR within approximately three days. The CMR will be attached to Battery "I".

18 July

4/12 continued arriving and establishing a position throughout the day.

52

DATE   ACTION

18 July   The Secretary of Defense, Mr. McNamara and the Ambassador to
(Cont)   Viet Nam Mr. Lodge were scheduled to pay a visit to the BLT, but
            a change of schedual cancelled this. However, the CO of RLT-7 did
            visit and toured the battery with LtCol. Taylor.

            Major Beatty and Capt. Harman went to Thuy Tan to fire smoke
            concentrations and register the howtars which will be laid with
            the primary direction of fire into the "A" Zone. Lt. Weld registered
            the 155's of "M" Battery from 225.

            Thuy Tan had 3 of their popular forces desert to the VC confirming
            that the VC have been in the area. Capt. Harman was asked to
            spend the night in the village but wisly declined since a Marine
            in Thuy Tan at night these days would stand the same chance as Mr.
            Johnson in the presidental suite of the Hanoi Hilton.

            Due to the increase of artillery as well as activity, LtCol. Taylor
            increased the volume of H&I fires for the 105's and 155's. Woe
            to the VC who didn't know about the 155's and pitched their
            shelter tents (or whatever it is they live in) just outside of
            105 range.

53

DATE	ACTION

18-20
July

4/12 completed its arrival and as a result the following officer changes have been effected: Lt. Rosenberg has become assistant S-3 with Lt. Cross as Bn FDO. Lt. Shaeffer has become Bn LnO and Lt. Statler will be the FDO. Additions to the battery include Lt. Threatte as FO for recon; Lt. Noble and Lt. Gustafson as FO's for I and L Companies respectivly. Lt. Guestafson will also relieve Lt. Schacht on hill 180 because the latter is returning to Okinawa to become ExO for "F" Battery there.

There have been a number of unusual incidents which have been a combination of bad luck, since they happened at all, and good luck, since the consequences were not more serious than they were. 4/12 had an accidental discharge which injured one man in the hand. Ontos also had an accidental discharge which sent a 106 round bouncing over HMM-161 to explode on the other side of the runway. That the round should bounce rather than explode on impact the first time it hit the ground in front of HMM-161 is unexplained. At any rate HMM-161 can claim to have been fired upon. HMM-161 was involved in the third incident when a helecopter went down, flipping over in the process, with 8 men from "M" Company aboard. Fortunately the only injury was a sprained back. As much equipment as possible was salvaged from the helecopter which was then blown up.

Le Dinh Sad, village chief for Thuy Tan complained that ducks were being poached from his form and asked for Capt. Harmans help. Capt. Harman visited the farm and inspected the evidence. Recon set up an ambush there but to no avail.

It had been expected that the BLT may be attacked on 20 July, but the predection did not materialize. Nevertheless, there was a considerable increase of action during that night. Thuy Phu had some activity causing Le Kim Bat to call in three concentrations which were Api Hai, Lei and Harman. Two popular forces were killed and one was listed as missing as a result of the skrimish 3 concentrations were also fired in Thuy Tan. There had been reports that the village of Phu Loung was being overrun, although these later proved to be exaggerated. However, an outpost had received mortar fire. Capt. Bao displaced two of his 155's to support the village, and his request that the BLT also displace 155's was denied. Two of our 155's were laid on the Thay bridge in Phu Loung and the 105's fired 3 HE and one illumination mission in support.

54

DATE	ACTION

18-20
July
(Cont)

The only major action within the TAOR involved a probing action of hill 225. At 2300 a trip flare was set off and a man was observed. He was fired at, but managed to escape. Lt. Weld called in a concentration using shell mixed to counter the threat. Again at about 0100 the hill was probed and this time the 155's fired the concentrations.

21-25
July

4/12 established itself in a permanent position, but as a result of an antenna farm constructed by 8th RRU, "M" Battery had to move to a new position between 8th RRU and the ARVN compound. The counter mortar radar unit is now situated on hill 180.

There was a meeting of the village chiefs of Thuy Tan, Thuy Phu and Thuy Loung at the BLT CP, which Major Zimmerman was introduced to the chiefs. This opportunity was taken to give the chiefs the helecopterride which had been promised by Capt. Harman. Capt. Harman accompanied the chiefs on the flight while Lt. Mullen, 3/4 S-1, went with the Popular Forces platoon commanders on another aircraft. The Vietnamese were all properly impressed by what was probably their first aerial flight.

A letter of recognition was presented to Capt. BAO, 12th ARVN Artillery, for the outstanding services he has performed on behalf of this battery. Afterwards, Capt. Bao, Major Beatty and Capt. Harman had lunch together. The whole affair was very gratifying for all concerned.

There has been a change of tactics within the BLT with sweeps now being held in the various routes of approach to the TAOR. One of these was held in Thuy Tan and Thuy Phu by recon, "L" and "M" Companies. The results were not spectacular but a number of suspects were detained and a quantity of rice uncovered.

H&I fires were conducted in the "A" zone by the howtar battery for the first time. The results were less than satisfactory as one of the villagers was hurt. There may be further repercussions from this incident. Battery "I" also experienced an unfortunate incident when Lt. Henderson attempted to fire a concentration with his own position being on the gun-target line. The rounds were supposed to be 600m from his position but unfortunately the initial rounds fell short and landed with 100m of the friendly front lines wounding a Marine from "M" Company. Fortunately the injury was not serious. In the future the 1000m rule will be strictly adhered to which is to say that initial rounds shall be at least 1000m from friendly positions.

A new draft arrived to the battery which included LCpl Dawkins and Kohut and Pvt. Hasdell. With the loss of so many men from outgoing drafts, these new men are greatly needed. SSgt Thomas has been transferred to Hq 4/12 to work in the FSCC.

55

DATE	ACTION
21-25 July Cont	General Walt and Col Wheeler were in the area to observe the new BLT tatics in action. A sweep was held with the 105's preparing the helecopter landing zone while the 155's fired diversionary fires into the jungle. The 155's were not too impressive, having four guns out of line. The artillery succeeded in scaring a large number of civilians out of the landing zone. A4D's then dropped an "L" shaped smoke pattern to designate the troop deployment limits which worked rather well. The sweep itself, however, brought forth no results.

LtCol. Taylor sent Capt Harman to Thuy Tan to establish liaision with Le Kim Bat and to await General Walt's arrival. When General Walt and Colonel Wheeler arrived, Le Kim Bat told them of the VC activity of 19 July. He took them to a vantage point at the Le Trac bridge and briefed them on the concentrations in the area. Lt. Davidson, Aide De Camp to General Walt took some pictures with a poloroid camera and the instant development process astounded the village chief.

The battery has been relieved of very little of its former responsibilities by 4/12. The permanent OP's on hills 180 and 225 are still manned by battery personnel and only the gunnery has been assumed by 4/12.

56

A
DATE   ACTION

26 July   This was a day to unravell problems the most complicated of which
              was the wounding of the Vietnamese civilian by the Howtar H&I fires.
              Major Beatty and Capt. Harman went to Thuy Tan to locate the crater
              of the shell that did the damage which turned out to be 1000m from
              its designated coordinates. Le Sin Sad, the village chief, took
              them to the home of the wounded man who is presently recovering
              in the hospital in Hue. The man is a widower with a 12 year old
              son. Captain Bao then took Major Beatty and Capt. Harman to the
              district chief where a 3000 piaster settlement was made. This will
              make it unnecessary to take further action through the civil affairs
              officer.

              Liberty continues in Hue with few incidents.

              PFC McClendon was awarded a Special Court Martial for insubordination
              which was the first such court in Battery "I" for 18 months.

              A liaision conference was held at Dong Da attended by LtCol Martin,
              Col Cu, ARVN Maj Beatty and Captain Harman, the purpose of which
              was to consider moving the CMR to Dong Da ammunition dump from hill
              180, but 1st Division vetoed the proposal because the radar might
              act as a conductor for lightening so the CMR is now located at the
              Battery "I" Motor Pool.

              Battery "I" has had the following attachments at one time or
              another since its arrival in Viet Nam.

                         A Tank Platoon
                         An Ontos Platoon
                         An Naval Gunfire Shore Fire Control Party.
                         An 81mm Mortar Platoon
                         A Counter Mortar Radar Unit.

              Few Battalions can make such a claim.

              The Battery also has an Aerial Observer capability with five
              Officers designated as technical observers. These officers have
              not been school trained but will become qualified as AO's after
              100 hours of flying experience.

              Capt. Harman and Sgt McCardle led Capt. Roach, CO of Battery "M"
              and Lt. Kuchenskos, CO of Howtar battery, on a reconnaissance of
              the forward artillery positions within the TAOR. The purpose was
              to show those officers the positions that their units will be
              occupying in the future.

57

DAY	ACTION

27 July   6 Missions were fired on suspected VC positions from hill 225.

LtCol Taylor desires to keep firing on hill 303 as intelligence indicates there is now possibly a division located in the area. As a result the 155 Battery will be moving forward to fire beyond hill 303 and the Howtar Battery will move to a position by hill 163 to cover the area around Ta Trach river.

The battery continues to prepare for the BLT CO's inspection on the 30th.

28 July   The TAOR has again been expanded to include the village of which is east of Phu-Bai.

It is expected that an additional regement will occupy the Phu-Bai area and will arrive sometime around September. In this event the TAOR will expand to the Loation border and westward to include the city of Hue.

The BLT will have an additional temporary committment of a company which will go to Da Nang, to guard the airstrip while the troops which ordinarily have that responsibility are on a sweeping operation.

General Walt, General Chuen and the American Consulate held a conference in Hue and the sxemplary conduct of the Marines while on liberty there was mentioned. Gen. Walt promised that a message of congradulations to the BLT for this conduct will be forthcoming.

4/12 has been busy firing in order to gain added gunnery experience. The Colonel has allowed them 200 rounds per day for this purpose although actual and suspected targets will be fired at when available.

Lt. Noble, from his OP on hill 153 spotted a group of about four VC enter the village at the base of hill 153. He called in fire on the village which was answered by both 105's and 155's. One round scored a direct hit on a building just after one of the VC entered. Surveillance could not determine casualties because the "L" Company Commander declined to cross the river (which is quite wide at that point) to search out the village.

29 July – 8 Aug   On 2 August at about 0700, Lt. Gustafson went with "I" Company to Da Nang to provide support for a sweep being held there. "I" Company replaced "C" 1/3 on the inner perimeter. Lt. Gustafson had his OP on hill 268. There were no incidents as far as "I" Company was concerned and Lt. Gustafson fired no missions. The sweep was quite successful, killing about 20 VC and capturing about 85. "I" Company returned to Phu Bai on the morining of 4 August.

Sgt c/for Gun #6

58

29 July –
8 Aug
(Cont)

Lt. Weld went with "K" Company on a similar mission to Chu Lai.
The company was flown down by GV, and upon arrival at the Chu Lai
airstrip, they proceeded to the positions in the inner peremeter
held by "K" 3/3. Meanwhile "K" 3/3 took up positions on the MLR,
"K" 3/4 had no incidents but "K" 3/3 had a man shot by the popular
forces. The next afternoon the company returned to Phu –Bai.

The battery has relinquished control of the OP's on hills 180 and
225 and the airport tower to 4/12. In the future the officers of
4/12 will man these OP's and communicators and equipment will be
provided by battalion. As far as Battery "I" is concerned, this is
the first constructive move made by 4/12 toward this unit. It
means, among other things, that the additional duties of the
Battery "I" Officers can and will be fulfilled.

LtCol. Rudzis talked to the Battery FO's, except for Lt. Weld who
was absent. He offered suggestions concerning FO tactics and
future plans were discussed.

Lt. Noble will become a permanent member of Battery "I" as a result
of a conference between Capt. Harman and LtCol. Rudzis over dinner.

Lt. Schaeffer and his liaision team at COC have often a tendency
to become the forgotten men" of Battery "I". However, Lt. Schaeffer
is one of the better FSC's and has constantly and energetically
worked for the good of the battery. For the 5th time he has drawn
up a target list for the TAOR. This is an indespensable item which
must be approved by LtCol. Taylor and LtCol. Rudzis as well as
Capt. Harman. The tact and deplomacy used by Lt. Schaeffer has
created a strong bond between the infantry and artillery and
completely fulfilled the liaision mission.

After many long months Naval Gunfire finally came into it's own.
The USS Galveston, a light cruiser arrived with 6 inch guns fired into
the area opposite hill 1154 with devastating effect. Unfortunately
Lt. Soechtig, the gunfire spotter, was languishing in the Air-
Conditioned ward at "A" Med with a neck infection and was unable
to adjust the fire. Instead an aerial observer, Lt. DeForrest, did
the adjusting from an L-19. Lt. Broesamle was helelifted off from
hill 180 on a minimum of notice to go to COC, there to perform the
liaision duties. He was joined by Sgt Wilder and the rest of the
liaision team. Lt. Broesamle's notice to leave hill 180 was so
minimal that an officer could not immediately be found to replace
him and, as a result; Capt. Harman spent the day on the hill.
LtCol Taylor observed the firing from a helecopter and was quite
impressed. Because of the large number of points from which to
obtain a navigational fix, the radar beacon was not utilized and the

59

DATE	ACTION

29 July –
8 Aug
(Cont)

beacon team has since returned to Da Nang. At the completion of
the exercise Lt. Broesamle was returned to his status of hermit
on hill 180. He did an excellent job as did his team but such are
the fortunes of war.

The Commandant of the Royal Thai Marine Corps, Semon Mesalac;
toured the TAOR and was briefed by Capt. Harman at gun #4 with the
counter-mortar board and the target list. Capt. Harman was followed
by Sgt. Carioty who gave a brief description of the gun emplacement.
Col Simmons, who is an artillery officer with JUSMAG in Thailand
was escorting officer for the Commandant. The colonel brought
regards from Col. Padley to Capt. Harman along with an invitation to
go on R&R in Bangkok. Since the Capt. has had liberty in Hue
only once, indications are that he will accept the invitation.

Col. Sherman, Chief of Staff of the 3d Marine Division replacing
Col. Lyman, toured 3/4. He was very much impressed by the Battery
"I" gun emplacements and wrote a personal note to Capt. Harman in
which he said that this was "one of the more professionally operated
field artillery batteries" that he had seen.

On Saturday the 31st of July "L" Company and recon company made a
sweep of the valley behind hill 163 and East of the Ta Trach river.
A CP group forward was established for this sweep and it included
LtCol. Taylor and LtCol. Rudzis. Lt. Weld was the FO with this CP
group. Upon completion of the area prep fires and the troop lifts
the CP group was helelifted to hill 163 where Lt. Weld set up his
OP. The howtar battery was helelifted to a position at the base of
hill 163. Lt. Weld fired a registration for the howtars and
simutaneously fired will adjust missions for Batteries "I" and "M".
The simutaneous missions were made possible by wire communications
with howtar battery and worked out very well. Lt. Weld fired a total of
3 missions for howtars, 5 for battery "M" and 2 for Battery "I" on
suspected enemy positions and avenues of approach. Zone fire was
used with good effect. The sweep itself produced negative contact
and the CP group returned by helecopter at about 1300. Details of
this operation from the COC standpoint are in the attached brief.

The "O" Club in the 3/4 area opened with festivities financed by
LtCol Taylor and free drinks for all. "Harman's Mob" made an
appearance after having had a private celebration in Capt. Harman's
tent during which 2 fifths of Beefeaters gin with Roses lime juice
were consumed. Missing from the celebration were Lt's. Soechtig,
Broesamle, Gustafson and Threatte who were in the hospital, on hill
180, in the field with "I" company and on hill 225 respectivly.

60

DATE	ACTION
29 July – 8 Aug (Cont)	In the absence of the Officer's, the battery was turned over to the Staff Non-Commissioned Officers.

Construction was begun on the new "E" Club. Upon completion it should be the biggest and best in the area, being 3 feet higher and 10 feet longer than any other. The cost of materials is being paid for by the men themselves at the rate of $2.00 per person. Wood and tin are purchased locally and so far $160.00 worth of wood and $100.00 of tin has been brought. Cement is obtained wherever possible, largely from the army. The club should be completed within ten days.

The battery is due to get some publicity on a national scale. General Walt sent Warrant Officer Smith, who is the division ISO, to do a story on the defensive fires for the villages in the TAOR. For this purpose Capt. Harman, Lt. Henderson and Sgt McCardle were interviewed. The article will stress the fact that these concentrations are unique in that they have been placed not primarily to kill but rather to discourage the VC and force them to break contact. For this reason the concentrations have been placed on the outskirts rather than within the village.

The defensive concentrations "A" through "E" in Thuy An Nang were fired using shell smoke with Major Webster, Major Baity and Capt. Harman being present. Although the firing of defensive concentrations in the past has been outstanding, this firing was, in the opinion of Capt. Harman, the best he had ever seen. The whole battery deserves the credit for the professionalism demonstrated by such results.

The battery experienced the best promotion period of the past 18 months. 10 men were promoted to Cpl while 16 made LCpl. The men promoted were.

E-4

PEARCE	VOORHEES
BOEHME	POTTER, K.
BAINO	MARLOW
LAMB	SUMMERS (NGF)
DESHANO	BRAWLEY (CHR)

E-3

SHARP	WADE	MULLER	WOLCOTT (NGF)
MCCLELLAN	JONES, R.K.	PENDLETON	ROWDEN (NGF)
REID	HANNAFIN	WOODHOUSE	DOMINGUEZ
SWARTHOUT	DAVIS	CATOE	DORNQUEST

R&R trips have been established for the battery with excursions to Hong Kong and Bangkok. The R&R is for a period of four days and is made under TAD orders. The trips will be awarded to the most

63

DATE	ACTION

29 July-
8 Aug
(Cont)

deserving personnel and will be controlled by the 1stSgt. Cpl Wilke and LCpl Davis went to Bangkok on 3 August while Cpl Baird and Cpl Barno made the trip on 9 August.

The CMR unit from 3/11 with GySgt Robinson as NCOIC and 12 men have been attached to Battery "I". It is interesting to note that a CMR unit is ordinarily a part of the regimental Headquarters Battery. The set is operational as demonstrated by the fact that it has successfully traced 81's and howtars. The sets are operated 24 hours a day and the 20° scan of which they are capable is laid between Thuy Loung and Thuy Phu.

The Battery has received 3 new men who are LCpl's Walsh, Autri and Wooldridge. However, the battery has lost one of its more valuable men in the person of HM3 "Doc" Francis, who departed to a new duty station in, of all places, Hawaii.

Lt. Weld took the big step and was sworn into the regular Marine Corps by Capt. Harman.

Major Baity departed 4/12 having been replaced by LtCol Rudzis as Commanding Officer. With the arrival of LtCol Rudzis, the officers of Battery "I" have had 7 reporting seniors since april. These have been, in order:

LtCol Jones	-	CO 3/4
LtCol Taylor	-	CO 3/4
LtCol Slack	-	CO 3/12
Major Gibney	-	CO 3/12
LtCol Page	-	CO 3/12
Major Baity	-	CO 4/12
LtCol Rudzis	-	CO 4/12

If this is not some sort of Marine Corps record it certainly ought to be.

Other officers who have come to 4/12 are the new executive officer, Major Webster and the S-3, Major Haesh.

4/12 continues to fire reinforcing type missions with the dual purpose of performing the normal artillery mission and the improvement of gunnery through constant practice. For the latter purpose, the BLT has authorized 4/12 an unlimited ammunition expenditure.

64

BRIEF ON OPERATION - SATURDAY 31 JULY 1965

Operation began at H-50 with AO adjusting fire on location of CP (Forward). Area was covered well.

At H-10 preparation began covering the LZ's and sweep area. AO reported that rounds were on target. Preparation was fired from 4 gun positions; 2 forward and 2 in CP area and consisted of 156 rounds of HE and 36 VT. Last 3 rounds fired were green smoke to indicate end of preparation and beginning of air strike.

There were 14 A4 jets on station. 8 of the jets made runs on the LZ's and surrounding area.

Immediately after the strike, 2 A4's laid smoke across the river, shielding the sweep LZ and area.

When smoke was completed troop lifts began. Lift was completed without incident.

Howtars and CP forward were then lifted to their respective forward positions without incident. Howtar lifted consisted of 19 chopper lifts.

Sweep made negative contact and sweeping unit was helilifted out at 1215.

Artillery (155, 105, 4.2) fired at no actual targets, but fired at suspected enemy positions all morning both for AO and FO (FO with CP (forward)).

65

DATE   ACTION

9-11 Aug   Major Heesch, Capt. Harman and W.O. Brown toured Thuy Loung, Tan, Phu and An Nang to check for possible communication problems but none were found. However, the village chief of Thuy Loung requested Marines to assist him in training his popular forces platoon.

Three 105mm howitzers have been deadlined as a result of enulsafred nitrogen in the recoil mechanism. Two of these have been replaced by "float" guns but a replacement has not been found for the third one. As a result the battery is operating with five howitzers.

The EM club is enough completed that it was opened on August 10th There is still some finishing up work to be done however. The club has three tables with benches that were constructed from ammo boxes. It has been decided to build tables and chairs rather than buy them. The money saved will be used to paint. Additional chairs still have to be built.

Liberty continues in Hue and in the "Chaplains House" is the name given to the combination bar and sporting house which has been built between Battery "I" and 3/4. The actual name is the Hong Kong Bar. The building is large, clean and nicely furnished. The drinks are of good quality but a little expensive (60 P for a mixed drink). The club employs about a dozen waiters and hostesses in addition to 10 prostitutes. The hostesses can be distinguished from the prostitutes by the fact that the latter ware short light blue dresses with numbers, 1-10, on them while the former wear ordinary street clothes. The hostesses do not engage in prostitution but merely provide companionship and encourage drinking. The prostitutes charge between $5.00 and $10.00, apparently depending upon what the customer will pay. The girls are not particularly solicitious and in fact seem a little independent. They are predominantly Chinese and not very attractive. Marines are permitted to wear civilian clothes in the club, but judging from the number there, it is doubtful that the club is experiencing any great financial success.

Lt. Beery has revamped the ammunition requirements so that the battery will now keep 1500 rounds in position rather than 700.

Da Nang received a second mortar attack and as a result, added emphasis has been placed on our CMR. It is the responsibility of the S-3 to inform the CMR of areas of possible mortar activity and assign a center of sector. Two guns from the battery are then laid in the direction of the possible mortar activity.

72

DATE	ACTION

9-11 Aug
(Cont)

LtCol. Rudzis toured the living areas of the battery. He found them satisfactory but suggested that drainage ditches be dug around all tents.

Construction in the battery area has included pouring concrete for the galley and erecting a new fly tent with a concrete slab for motor transport.

Lt. Noble went with 1 platoon of recon to set up a night ambush along the Song Nang near An Cu. They observed two men across the river and fired upon them but did not hit them. Lt. Weld and Lt. Gustafson also went with their companies to set up ambushes in the same area, but neither had any activity.

On Aug 10th Lt. Henderson went on a patrol with the 3d Platoon of recon company. The mission was to find a route of approach for tanks to the base of hill 303 for a future sweep which will involve tanks, artillery and infantry. The secondary mission was to find a route of approach for "M" Company. Recon was helelifted to hill 42 at 0600 and patrolled toward hill 303 arriving at 1030. They succeeded in finding a route of approach along a creek bed. After about an hours rest the patrol moved east to the Song Nang and found a secondary route of approach. While returning to base camp the patrol detained 7 VC suspects. COC instructed them to escort the suspects out of the TAOR. The patrol returned to base camp at about 1800. The distance covered by the patrol was over 20,000 meters, and much of this was without a resupply of water because the creeks which were to be used were dried up.

12 Aug

A special court martial convened for the case of PFC McClendon who was charged with disrespect to a Non-Commissioned Officer. He was found guilty and received 3 months confinement and loss of 2/3 pay for 3 months.

LtCol. Taylor visited the newly opened and yet un-named Battery "I" EM Club.

The officers moved out of their old obsolete BOQ and into the ordnance tent across the way. Then they helped Cpl Marlow move out of his ordnance tent and into the old, obsolete BOQ. However, the BOQ which is now the ordnance tent was made less obsolete by the addition of a new, raised deck. For this task, Cpl Marlow also received help from the officers.

At about 1857 while on an enemy recon flight, Lt. J. D. Richards, a division AO, received small arms fire from the vicinity of coordinates 795064 and 803058. This is the area across the Song Ta Trach near hills 153 and 163 where there has been considerable VC activity lately. Lt Richards called in a fire mission which was fired by "M" Battery. He received 3 fire for effects with excellent effect on the target area. However, Lt. Richards could still see 73

DATE	ACTION

12 Aug
(Cont)
people on the ground and muzzle blasts from their weapons. Therefore, he shifted right 100 and fired for effect again. At 1930, he left the area because the firing was getting heavy and there was considerable danger to the aircraft, an L-19. While flying north he received more small arms fire from vicinity coordinates 815125, but continued back to the airfield landing at about 1930. The artillery LnO then called in a fire for effect mission using shell mixed and zone fire on the area. This was accomplished at 1945. "M" battery continued to fire the zone fire periodically through the evening. Mortgage 3 also requested zone fire three times during the night on the area from which the small arms fire initially came.

13 Aug
Movies are now being shown in the battery area whenever the film and generator are available. During the showing of Fanny, which was the best movie to date, the projector bulb burned out after $2\frac{1}{2}$ reels so nobody could see the end of the picture. Happy friday the 13th.

Lt Weld was helelifted with "K" Company to hill 69 at about 1700. The set up a night defensive position and two squad size ambushes. Lt Weld made a coordinated fire plan with 81mm mortars which were attached. The 81's fired close in concentrations and Lt Weld fired two will adjust missions with 105's on avenues of approach. He also made recommendations for H&I fires. There was no VC activity and the company returned at about 0700.

14 Aug
Meetings at 3/4 which had been every day will now be on Mondays Wednesdays and Fridays. This will also apply to the battery meetings.

Construction work for the monsoon season continues.

An unfortunate accident occurred when a man from "M" Company was badly burned while washing his mess gear. Kerosine from the emersion burner got on his clothes and caught fire. The man panicked and began to run, but thinking quickly Cpl Lamb tackled the man and put out the fire with sand. The man had 2nd degree burns on chest and legs and had to be evacuated. Cpl Lamb's quick action undoubtably saved him from even more serious injuries.

Lt. Soechtig acted as an FO for howtar battery during a service shoot. The howtars fired from the area by the tin shack while Lt Soechtig had his OP about 1200m forward.

Lt Henderson went on a night patrol and ambush with the 3d platoon of C recon company. They established an ambush on the road to Lang Xa in an attempt to catch any individuals attempting to use the area. One Marine threw a grenade into a bush but the area in which he threw it was lower than the area where he was laying down

74

DATE	ACTION

14 Aug (Cont)
As a result he caught some shrapnel in his head which required 10 stitches. This was the only "action" of the night.

15 Aug
Lt Gustafson went with "I" company to Da Nang on 11 Aug for 4 days to replace "F" company 2/3 which participated in the first night Marine offensive in Viet Nam. There were intelligence reports that indicated that Da Nang may be mortared sometime during that period. The mortar fire was not received, however, until the evening after "I" company departed.

At 0600 Lt Beery and GySgt Brewer took one gun out to the oasis to fire concentrations in preparation for a forthcoming operation. They fired 20 rounds in three missions, returning to the battery at 0930.

At 1600 Lt Weld went by truck with "K" Company to hill 36. At 0400 they were supposed to participate in an operation with the ARVN and popular forces with the ARVN sweeping north of RT#1 toward the highway and "K" company setting up a blocking force there. However, the ARVN were committed elsewhere during the night and were not available for the operation. Lt Weld reported seeing young men (16 to 25 years old) working in the fields. This is the first time he has ever noticed this.

16 Aug
Today was pay day and the night before Capt Bao called Capt Harman and asked if he could obtain some american money through the sale of piasters. Capt Harman replied this would be possible since the troops need the piasters and Capt Bao was offering 110 to the dollar which is higher than can be obtained in Hue. At about 0600 Capt Bao showed up in Capt Harman's tent with $1500 in piasters which is enough to fill a good sized suitcase. This was a few more piasters than was anticipated (like about $1300 more) even so the battery brought about $700 worth.

A 105mm howitzer was sent to Da Nang to have its recoil mechanism replaced.

An excellent article was written about Battery "I" in the Stars and Stripes. The article was written by WO Jim Smith and was about 500 words long. It was titled Leatherneck Artillery Serves Twofold Purpose in Viet Nam, and concerned the defensive concentrations in the Phu-Bai village complex. A picture of Gen Walt, LtCol Taylor Capt. Harman and Le Kim Bat accompanied the article.

The battery held a night RSOP and occupation of position in preparation for the forthcoming operation behind hill 303. The recon group went out at about 1800 to set up the position. The battery followed at 2000 and was in position at 2033. The guns were laid and ready to fire at 2045. The battery fired 4 H&I missions for a total of 20 rounds and returned at about 2130.

75

DATE	ACTION
17 Aug	Capt Harman, Capt Hanschey, USA, Sgt Tong, ARVN, Lt Soechtig and Sgt McCardle went to An Nang to fire in concentrations A,B,C,D,E and F for village chief Hau. The initial rounds all landed within 50 meters of the target and in one case within 50 meters of a civilian who immediatly took steps, long and rapid ones, to increase that distance. Chief Hau promised Capt. Harman a dog for a pet. If somebody offers the capt a water banffalo he will then have a complete cross-section of Vietnamese domestic animals (dogs, goats and water buffaloes).

Lt Soechtig was scheduled to go with recon on an ambush at Ain Chu. However, the scheduled helecopters did not arrive and the operation had to be ambushed.

Intelligence dictates that 3/4 may be hit by 2 or 3 battalions of VC sometime between the 18th and 20th. Therefore the operation behind hill 303 which was scheduled for the 18th has been cancelled. Chu Lai and Da Nang are also expecting action and for this reason "L" Company has been sent to Chu Lai.

18 Aug	The battalion prepared for a visit by Gen Krulak with the artillery practing massing fires on a target. However, an operation at Chu Lai caused the generals visit to be postponed. All was not in vain because the village chiefs and popular forces sergeants were present for the generals visit and witnessed the artillery demonstration.

As a result of the intelligence which indicates 2 or 3 VC battalions in the area, all units have been put on 50% alert. This situation will exist for five or ten days.

The battery area is now completely surrounded by a barbed wire fence. There is also a gate which sports a sign reading "IN HARMANS HUE".

The Capt little goat which has now grown rather large, broke his leg and is now hobbling around in a splint.

Lt Statler is now on hill 225 from where he called a fire mission on a water buffalo, killing same. Lt Soechtig went out with a platoon of recon company to set up a night ambush west of Lang Xa. They did not see any VC.

Lt. Henderson went with "M" Company to sit up a night ambush beyond hill 46. They had no contact either.

76

DATE	ACTION
19 Aug	Gen Krulak showed up for an unexpected visit at 1500. The Officers and Staff gathered at "A" Med to hear a briefing by the 3/4 officers and a short talk by Gen Krulak. A vase made from the first shell fired on the Phu Bai village defensive concentrations was presented to the Gen which he appreciated very much (See attached details). The S-2 and S-3 summed up the tactical situation since the General's last visit and Lt Eck briefed him on the platoons that have been working with the popular forces in the villages. He emphasized the increase of intelligence information from the villagers as a result of this project. LtCol Taylor made a special point of mentioning the fine job that the artillery has continued to do.

In his talk Gen Krulak emphasized the importance of the fighting that the BLT has been doing even though little actual combat has been involved. He also mentioned that there are now more Marines in Viet Nam than there ever were in Korea. Perhaps the most interesting information that the Gen had to give concerned an operation at Chu Lai which was in progress. A full regiment of VC were known to be on a penensula about 15 miles south of Chu Lai. It was decided to attack them before they could attack the airbase. The entire operation was planned in three days. One battalion was landed by sea, a company went overland as a blocking force and the SIF from the Iwo Jima was loaded by air. The Marines had killed about 500 VC although an accurate count could not be made because the battle was still in progress. Marine casualties were about 20 KIA and 130 WIA; 75% of the WIA were superficial wounds. This is the biggest battle fought in Viet Nam to date.

After his talk, Gen Krulak went to 4/12 where an artillery demonstration with Capt. Bao as OIC was conducted. Five Batteries, 2 ARVN and 3 USMC were involved, with Capt Bao firing the howitzers located at Nan Hoa. The FO was one of Capt. Bao's officers, Lt. Son. After the demonstration, Gen Krulak presented Capt Bao with a USMC pin, and Capt Bao was very much impressed by this gesture.

A counter mortar drill was held during the evening with a reaction time of 3 minutes. Chief Hon of An Nang village later called in an illumination mission an concentration A and D. Reaction time for this was only 1½ minutes.

The fact that the battery has been on 50% alert is partially responsible for these reaction times.

Lt. Henderson went with "M" Company to conduct patrols and ambushes in the oasis area but had no contact.

77

DATE	ACTION
22-29 Aug	Females have been prevalent in the battery this week.

Capt Bao has 2 female goats in need of male companionship. Capt. Harman has an extra male goat which would appreciate female companionship. Therefore, an arrangement was made which should produce little goats in about six months.

The battery also has four dogs, all females, 2 of which belong to Headquarters and 2 of which belong to the galley. The Hq dogs are named dog, which is appropriate and Charlie, which is not so appropriate for a female at least the galley dogs are named zero and tilt, both good dog names.

There has been an increase of rats in the area, due to the change in climate. These will have to be poisoned, even though the poison will constitute a danger to the dogs.

General Krulak sent Capt Harman a picture for Capt Bao which shows Capt Bao and General Krulak together during the artillery demonstration. Col Taylor also gave Capt Harman a copy of the picture which accompanied the newspaper article on Battery "I". It was signed by LtCol Taylor and had the inscription, "Thanks for the best battery in the Corps" - Woody Taylor.

August 25th was Capt Harmans birthday and 1stSgt Satterfield gave a little party with pink champaign. A cake was also presented later on in the club.

There is no liberty in Hue until further notice due to student riots there. The riots were caused by the government wanting to draft the professors at the university and are both anti american and anti Vietnamese. Therefore, they are pro-Comunist.

The monsoon season has begun to arrive with two straight days of rain. Capt Harmans super highway and culvert system is having a little trouble, but repair work continues.

Cpl Barno's extension in Viet Nam has been approved. That is well because he is an importaint man to the battery. He is combination battery business NCO, finance NCO, non-official requisition NCO and driver. He could also be called the morale NCO because he is primarily responsible for procurring beer, soda and ice. Without these items, morale would indeed go down. No matter how difficult the gear is to get, Cpl Barno can be counted on to get it, although he has been ambushed and shot at a number of times in the process. Where and how he finds these things is a trade secret.

66

DATE	ACTION

22-29
Aug
(Cont)

Sgt Wilder and Cpl Richardson left on the September Draft. Cpl Padilla applied for an extension.

The naval gunfire section has been put on alert to move to Chu Lai. This section has done a great deal of work for the battery, little of which concerned naval gunfire, but all of which has been appreciated.

Lt. Soechtig replaced Lt. Statler on hill 225. While Lt. Statler was on 225 a cobra was killed there. Apparently the damp weather has been driving the snakes to higher ground. It rains almost every day on 225 and, unfortunately the bunkers leak making for much disconfort.

Lt. Noble and LCpl Reid returned from Chu Lai. They did not see action in the battle there but brought back some interesting stories. It seems that H Company 2/4 landed right next to the VC regimental CP and got into a firece fight giving and receiving many casualties. LtCol Fisher distingusihed himself by a display of personal leadership and courage. When troops fired into straw houses, and the straw was shot away it was revealed that concrete bunkers were built inside the houses. These fortified positions had to be taken in the same manner that similar positions were taken during the battle for Okinawa.

Lt. Henderson went out with "M" Company and did much patrolling and setting up of ambushes but with no real results.

Cpl Lamb went with 2nd platoon recon to hill 153 where they set up an OP and observed groups of 2 and 3 VC in the area. At about 1800 they they observed 8 VC enter a hut and received permission to fire on it. The initial rounds landed short but the following rounds scored 3 direct hits.

LCpl Cato went with 3rd platoon of recon and set up OP's on hill 163. at about 1000 they observed 12 VC with automatic weapons and helmets walking near the river. LCpl Catoe called in fire which caused the VC to run into the brush along the river. Catoe then fired into the brush, neutralizing the area throughly. He thought he got all 12 VC but they were not permitted to search for bodies.

Lt Gustafson went on a 2 day patrol with recon along the eastern edge of the TAOR. They went to the edge of the jungle and penetrated slightly. During the patrol they detained a couple of civilians as VC suspects.

LCpl Hannifin went on an ambush with recon about 4000m north of hill 36. The ambush was set along a road with listening posts set forward.

67

DATE	ACTION

22-29 Aug (Cont)

The listening posts signalled that a squad sized VC patrol was approaching. When the patrol was within 5 feet of the ambush, recon opened fire. The VC ran straight into the ambush and jumped over it. One man from recon shot 2 of them in mid-air. (Three more and he will be an ace). The ambush killed 5 and departed the area. The next morning they returned and 3 bodies were still there as well as a considerable quantity of equipment.

The big operation for the week was Jungle Foot. "L" Company, "M" Company and Recon Company participated as well as all of the artillery units. "M" and Recon Companies swept the jungle area behind hill 303 followed by "L" Company. The artillery fired barrier fires which were adjusted by Lt. Soechtig from 225. Battery "I" didplaced for the operation to the Oasis at 2400 on D-1 arriving at 0120. 302 rounds of pre-planned barrier fires were fired and the battery returned to the base camp at 1300. The operation did not trap any VC however.

The battery fired a high burst registration which was observed by Lt. Soechtig from Hill 225 and Lt. Moran from hill 180.

Lt. Walker replaced Lt. Soechtig on hill 225 as the latter could prepare to move to Chu Lai with the Naval Gunfire Section.

Lt. Noble departed the battery to become the XO of "M" Battery. He was replaced by Lt. Andrea.

Capt. Harman procurred a dump truck from Capt. Bao to help work on the road for the big battle against the rain.

A pleasant sight occurred fro the battery when a pretty Vietnamese girl accompanied by her boyfriend drove right through the battery position. They were looking for someone to buy ice. Capt. Harman offered them sodas but brought no ice.

30 Aug 1 Sep

A Sony Stereo Tape Recorder was purchased for the "E" Club.

3 guns displaced to firing point 6 by the tin shack for a service practice shoot. 180 rounds were fired and were adjusted by the FO's on hills 180 and 225.

Generals Wade and Henderson toured the BLT area on 31 August but did not visit the Battery "I" area. The battery had been preparing for a visit by the regimental commander on the 31st but he did not arrive until the next day. The Col said that Battery "I" was living up to its outstanding reputation.

A meritorious mast was awarded to Sgt McCardle for outstanding performance of duty by LtCol Rudsiz. It was presented at evening formation. The mast cited Sgt McCardle for the outstanding survey which he has accomplished since the batterys arrival in Viet Nam.

68

DATE	ACTION

30 Aug
1 Sep
(Cont)

Personnel will now be paid in MPC. After 30 September it will be illegal to possess american currency. The MPC may be exchanged for piastes at the rate of 118 piastas per dollar.

3 new men arrived in the Battery. They are PFC's Scott and Pesta LCpl FICETOLA. Scott and Ficetola wereassigned to the NGF section while Pesta will work in supply.

Lt. Anderer fired 2 missions at 3 VC in the area of hill 107. A surveillance could not be made due to the jungle area.

Lt. Gustafson spent two nights out with "I" Company but had no activity.

A new FO list has been established as follows: Lt Weld, "K" Co, Lt Henderson, "M" Co, Lt Gustafson, "I" Co, Lt Anderer, "L" Co and Cpl Marlatt, Recon Co.

4 VC were discovered at HMM-161 and fired at by a sentry but escaped.

A squad from Lt. Ecks platoon picked up 4 VC suspects in Phu-Bai village. One confessed under interrogation in Hue. The other 3 had to be brought to Da Nang. They finally confessed because they were blindfolded and didn't know where they were. It is apparently important to the VC to know where they are before they die.

2 Sep

It would appear that higher headquarters either has great confidence or little interest in Battery "I" since Col. Calendar was only the forth artillery visitor in over four months. LtCol. Slack visited once on the 20th of April and Col. Pala and Maj Gibney also paid short visits. All other visitors have been from the infantry.

Naval Gunfire will definately be remaining with the battery after many false alarms. They will be particularly useful to the Comm section as they have in the past and of course there are always working parties. Some day they may even fire naval gunfire again.

Lt. Smith of "M" Battery went out with recon on a 48 hour ambush to the S.E. portion of the TAOR. They observed 50 persons moving down a stream bed and seeming to be carrying something. It was possible that they were in uniform and armed. They did a good job of observing but no shooting.

Cpl Marlow's brother who is in the Airforce and is stationed in Saigon is visiting the battery for a couple of days.

Lt Ecks platoon brought in 3 more VC prisoners. One is alledgedly the chairman of the local communist organization. They will be transferred to Da Nang.

69

DATE	ACTION

2 Sep
(Cont)

The men were paid in MPC's today. The legal rate of exchange for piasters is 118 per MPC dollar. The rate of exchange for greenbacks is about 10 years.

Liberty begins in Hue again tomorrow for men who have enough piasters to afford it. It is, of course, not legal to exchange MPC's for P's except in authorized places (which do not include cyclo boys) and there is a shortage of P's at present.

3 Sep

Today, was a particularly quiet day in that the guns did not fire a single mission.

Capt. Harman invited Capt. Bao and his Officers for a tour of the battery position.

Greenbacks are now being turned in in exchange for MPC's.

R&R trips have been cancelled due to lack of flights.

Lt. Weld went with "K" Company to the vicinity of hill 153. His platoon set out two squad ambushes leaving only one for the CP group which isn't conducive to sound sleeping. No contact was made.

4 Sep

3 guns went to the area around the tin shack for a service practice shoot. 133 rounds were fired.

Capt Harman and Lt Henderson attended a dinner at 12th ARVN with Capt Bao.

Cpl Marlow's brother returned to Saigon.

Sgt Duke ₍APFC RECO₎ came to Battery "I" from Hq 4/12 and will work in ordnance.

At about dusk, "K" Company was moving west from hill 36 to the objective area and spotted about a platoon of VC. They engaged them in a fire fight during which Lt. Stenick was hit in the head and another man in the throat. Both casualties are serious and had to be evacuated but will apparently survive. A sweep was made the next morning and blood trails were found but no bodies. *It also was* *~~~~~~~~~~*

At about 1800 recon spotted 20 VC near the area of hill 207. They had rifles and were carrying supplies. Cpl Summers called in a mission which took 45 minutes to be fired and by that time the VC were 1500m away. By this time "K" Company had been hit and OP Tango would not except corrections to adjust fire onto the target. So Cpl Summers fired on a river crossing that they used but by this time it was too dark to see the effect.

70

DATE	ACTION

4 Sep
(Cont)

At about 0430 H&S(-); "I" Company and 2 platoons from joint reaction force provided a blocking force on route #1 north of Da Nang for a sweeping force of 9 platoons from Dongda. They swept An Loung and picked up 43 suspects.

There are now double pipes in the culverts perhaps they will hold up under the rains.

Lt Henderson is now disk jockey in charge of the club tape recorder.

The battery is playing musical officers with Lts Anderer, Walker and Weld due to leave.

LtCol. Taylor advised Capt. Harman to allow cows to graze in the ravine by his tent between 0800 and 1800. There is a young cowherder named Bao who the Capt has semi-adopted. He has given the boy a toothbrush.

We also have goats mating in the area.

71

DATE	ACTION

7-8Sep   Lt. Soechtig, Cpl Summers and Pvt Gentile accompanied a recon platoon to hill 153 to set up an OP. They arrived at nightfall of the 5th and set in position. During the night a hot fire fight was observed between the ARVN and the VC. The next morning the ARVN were still sweeping the area and did not leave until about 0800. At about 1100 Lt. Soechtig spotted a squad of VC entering the area, but they could not be observed for a long enough period to bring them under fire. It was decided to let them enter and keep them under observation rather than fire ineffectivly and put them on the alert. The area was kept under observation during the day with occasional spottings of suspicious personnel. At about 1700, patience paid off when the VC exposed themselves again. About four of them seemed to be observing the OP so it was decided that the time had come to take them under fire. A mission was called using a shift from a previous plotted concentration. Before the first round was on the way, more VC appeared and apparently suspected that they were under observation because they were attempting to sneak out of the area. There were about 20 and they were moving eastward in column formation along draws and wooded areas. The first round landed far to the west of them and caused them to speed up their retreat, a left 1000 brought the 2nd round to their east and caused them to slow down and think things over. The third round landed very close to them as they continued to move eastward. They went into a draw and the fire for effect went in with them. Two bodies were observed to be thrown into the air and the fire for effect was such that 10 casualties were estimated. 2 VC appeared from the draw and a repeat fire for effect was given. They were seen no more. The area was kept under surveillance for about 20 minutes with no more sightings except for a single individual running like mad to the south about 500m from the area. Lt. Holmann, the platoon commander then decided to vacate the area as it was believed the position was compromised, before leaving a mission was fired on a couple of VC who were spotted in an open area near a house. The first rounds sent them into the brush. The second rounds sent them one of them out and into the brush on the other side of the field. The fire for effect entered the area where the VC had run but he was not sighted again so a positive surveillance could not be made. The patrol then left 153 and was picked up by helecopters for return to base camp. It is interesting to note that Lt. Weld who had just that day left Btry "I" to become FDO for 4.2 battery was the FDO for these missions. This was Lt. Welds first watch in the battalion FDC and he handled it very proffessionally.

Other officer changes included the departure of Lt. Walker to become 4.2 XO and Lt. Anderer to become battalion survey/metro officer. Lt. Anderer replaced Lt. Rosenberg who has become an advisor at Da Nang. Cavagnol and Booth came to Battery "I" to become FO's for recon, "L" Co and "K" Co respectivly. Lt Smith will be Recon FO but remains at "M" Battery. On the night of the 5th Lt. Weld went out with K Company to the area where the fire fight occurred on the fourth. One squad spotted approximately 40

83

DATE	ACTION

7-8Sep
(Cont)

VC coming down the road. However, before word could be brought back to Capt. Marino, the VC had disappeared from sight, so no action could be taken.

Since August 21 at least 192 VC have been observed in about a dozen seperate sightings. Activity is thickening.

On the 8th, 3 guns went out to firing point 3 to provide supporting fires for the ARVN forces.

Captain Harman and Major Webster went on a tour of the TAOR. They touched down on hill 180, where Lt. Statler has been since Sunday, and 225. It was decided that the bunker on hill 225 is adequate but the one on hill 180 needs work.

Lt. Cross returned from an R&R trip to Hong Kong.

It was not mentioned earlier that Lt. Weld was hit during the fire fight on the night of 4 September. He was grazed in the elbow be a bullet or fragment. The wound was not so serious as to see the medical officer, but is necesary to have the Corpsman bandage it. This particular fire fight had been a fairly hot one with the VC employing accurate automatic weapons fire. However, our machine guns, 3.5 rockets and M-79 proved too much for them.

The speed limit in Viet Nam has been reduced to 20 MPH.

5 M-35's will be deadlined in preparation for a CG's inspection on 14 October.

There has been a change in fire commands. In the future 1 gun is a section, 2 guns a platoon and 3 or more a battery.

Lt F. L. Henderson the AO spotted 3 VC crossing the river near hill 153 on a log while he was on a recon flight. He called in a mission and battery "M" fired 24 rounds while battery "I" fired 14. He got a direct hit on the log giving the VC an acute splinter problem.

Lt. Henderson of Battery "I" is in A Med with ameobic dysentary.

9-12Sep

On 10 September a joint operation was held with ARVN to sweep the villages on both sides of the river by hill 153. Lt Cavagnol was FO for L Company. Lt. Smith FO for recon and Lt. Soechtig and Booth were FO's for the 192nd Company of ARVN regional forces. The operation began on the night of the 9th with recon and L Company patrolling the area near 153. Lt's Soechtig and Booth went to the MACV compound in Hue to meet the ARVN advisors Capt Fury, USA and WO Dicky, Australian army. From there they went to the district

84

DATE | ACTION

9-12Sep
(Cont)

Headquarters where they spent the night. Lts Soechtig and Booth brought two full FO teams which included Cpls Lamb and Marlatt although only one was actually required. At daybreak "L" Company took up a blocking position at the base of 153 while recon began sweeping the village. Lt Smith sent his scout sergeant, Cpl Summers to the top of 153 to establish an OP. Meanwhile ARVN took up a blocking position in the village across the river. Recon's sweep resulted in the detention of a large number of civilians and the village was burned and blown up. The ARVN sweep revealed nothing. On two of the artillery missions fired there were errors which resulted in rounds being fired 1000 and 2000 meters from target. One fell near recon and another near Cpl Summers OP. One of the rounds was caused by a 200 m error on the guns ("M" Battery) but the reason for the other could not be determined. The operation ended at about 1400.

While the above operation was in progress a company of VC attempted to over-run an ARVN outpost east of Phu Bai. Apparently they thought that the artillery had displaced all of its guns. They were wrong because Battery "I" had left 2 guns behind. A mission was called in and all hands who were still in the area had to man the guns. It took just three minutes to shift trails and get out the first round. In all, 50 rounds of VT were fired. The initial rounds hit right on target but a total surveilance could not be made.

Lt. Gustafson returned from Chu Lai. While there with Co "I" they helped man the perimeter and took part in patrols around the inner TAOR. He also took part in a sweeping operation. Upon debarking from LVT's at the position from which the sweep was to begin a mine was set off wounding 5 men. Later the Company took small arms fire while occupying a blocking position on a hill. Lt Gustafson fired artillery on the snipers but a surveilance could not be made. The company then swept through a village picking up all men of military age. The women of the village staged a protest demonstration but it had no effect. Upon completion of this operation, the company was immediately dispatched to a blocking position in front of the lines. There was no activity in this position. The company was supposed to return to Phu Bai on 10 September but instead had to occupy the airfield perimeter in place of 3/3 who went to Da Nang. They returned on 11 September 1965.

On the night of the 11th Lt Cavagnol went with a platoon of L Co to an ambush at hill 70; Cpl Summers went to highway 14 with recon and Lt Gustafson went to An Cu with I Co. There was no action reported by any of these units.

The "E" club was officially opened on the 11th of September. The club has been named "Tuns Tavern-Phu Bai". Inside the club,

85

DATE   ACTION

9-12Sep
(Cont)   bulletin boards have been installed on which are posted information
              of interest to battery "I". Among the dignitaries attending the
              opening were LtCol Rudzis and Taylor, and Capt Bao. The club was
              packed to capacity. 24 cases of beer were sold and a great quantity
              of soda as sell. There was popcorn, crackers and cheese, pastry as
              well as two large cakes baked especially for the occasion.

              On the 11th Gen Waters, USA and Gen. Walt visited the 3/4 area.

              LtCol Muir, CO of 1/1 ~~was assassinated by a VC suicide squad at~~
              ~~Da Nang.~~

              Gen Mangrum, the assistant Commandant visited Phu Bai. An artillery
              demonstration was conducted with the battalion massing fires.

              Maj Watson visited Capt Harman. He is now Headquarters Commandant
              for division in Da Nang.

13Sep   Lt Booth went out with K Company to set up an ambush on highway 14.
              The ambush utilized grenades set off be detonating cord on the
              opposite side of the road including the usual small arms. The whole
              thing was triggered by 3 women and a boy. It was a traumatic
              experience for them but amazingly they were not hurt. What they
              were doing out after curfew is not known but it is suspected that
              they were bringing supplies to VC in the jungle. As a result the
              four were brought in for questioning.

              Lt. Smith has been operating with recon in the area of hill 153.
              He had an OP set up on the forward slope of 163 and was observing
              activity in the general area. At about 1730 he observed two men
              who seemed to be carrying objects, one long and tubular and one
              round and flat. They went into a banana patch near a blue house
              and put the two objects together. This spells mortars so Lt. Smith
              called in a fire mission. He adjusted the rounds into the area
              where he observed the two men and fired for effect. One came
              running out as he repeated fire for effect. He saw no further
              sign of men or mortar.

              At present the battalion is keeping one company at Da Nang. It will
              be policy to keep the remaining three companies on the line putting
              a platoon from one on hill 225 and a platoon from each of the others
              in the field. Therefore, there will be two FO's one with each
              field platoon, in the field at all times. Recon is sending 2
              platoons to Chu Lai, leaving one behind so there will still be a need
              for a recon FO.

              The battery lost a volleyball and poker player as well as a good
              Staff NCO because SSgt Hollier has been transferred to battery "M"
              SSgt Moulico will replace him.

                                                                    86

DATE	ACTION

13Sep
(Cont)

Nobody will be permitted to make a run to Hue without permission from the 1stSgt or Capt Harman due to the increased possibly of vehicles being ambushed.

The people to people program will continue with aid being given to the Vietnamese people by the Corpsman. Doc Blight and Doc Snyder will take part in this.

A Lt (USN) from the Seabees visited the area to check requirements. He promised that in the near future (Mabe Nov) a 16x64 ft galley would be built as well as all tents strongbacked.

14-15Sep

The long expected and awaited monsoon season has arrived with 48 hours of rain and no let-up in sight. The battery road has some difficulty when a culvert collapsed. This was repaired along with some minor erosion damage. The road will survive...or else. To counter-act erosion damage to the sloped sides of the gun pits, sod is being procured from 12th ARVN and is being placed on the sides. All in all the rain did no great damage, but did point out a few weaknesses in preparation which must be corrected.

A service practice shoot was scheduled for the 15th. Lt Soechtig took a tema up to hill 180 to act as an FO. However, the rain got so bad that the shoot had to be secured.

An FDO xk school is being held for lieutenants at A/12. It is run informally without an attendance being taken because of field committments.

Capt Harman rounded up two goats for Capt Bao. One is for stud service and the other for fattening up.

A mess night was held on the night of the 15th at 4/12. LtCol Taylor was the guest of honor. Attending from Btry "I" were Lt's Schaeffer, Gustafson, Cavagnol, Booth and Soechtig as well as Capt Harman. The mess night featured everything a normal one would except dress uniform. There were even not one, but two kinds of wine. It is planned that a mess night shall be held each month. LtCol. Taylor said that he hoped 3/4 could retaliate.

16-19Sep

On 12 Sept the battery fired its 10000th round since arriving in Viet Nam. Cpl Potter was the section chief for the gun which fired the round. The round was fired during the demonstration for Gen Mangrum.

Cpl Summers spent a night with the battalion scouts on hill 139 which is within spitting distance of hill 180. They did not see anything.

Lt. Booth went out with "K" Company near An Cu. While crossing the Song Nang a man from K Company was drowned. Lt Booth fired continuous illumination to aid the rescue efforts. The body could not be recovered until the next day when members of the popular forces arrived in Sanpans to aid with the diving ef.

87

DATE	ACTION
16-19Sep Cont	efforts.

Lt. Smith with a platoon from C recon made contact with the VC near hill 153. The VC were first observed on 153. They moved down the slope and recon engaged them in a fire fight Lt. Smith called in artillery and walked the rounds into the VC position. The VC broke contact and Lt. Smith fired artillery into suspected VC positions. A physical reconnaissance of the area turned up blood trails indicating some number of casualties.

Doc Blight made E-4 and brought the battery 100 cans of beer.

The battery displaced 3 guns to firing point 6 for a practice shoot. However, instead of practicing, they fired at actual VC for Lt. Smith.

M-109 Self-propelled 155 mm howitzers arrived at Phu Bai. As a result of their arrival., Battery "I" is due to receive two of the 155 towed howitzers. About 20 men from the battery went to 4/12 to look at the new weapons.

It is currently rumored that the howtar battery will move down to Da Nang.

The 81mm mortars which had been set up near the battery have moved back to 3/4

The 1st Marine Division has arrived on Okinawa. Rumor has it that they will come to Viet Nam sometime before the end of the year. What effect this will have on the status of the 3d Marine Division can only be guessed.

The CO of M Company Capt Rycliff was relieved for cause at Da Nang and will be replaced by Capt. Keenan.

Close defensive concentrations are being planned around the battalion area, and are being fired in with smoke rounds. To date concentrations for Co L and Co K have been fired in and cover the eastern half of the area from the middle of the airport to the middle of the 3/4 area. The first to be fired were for K company when Capt Harman and Capt. Marine went out to observe the rounds. Later, L Company's were fired and these were also witnessed by Maj Webster, Lt Cavagnol acted as FO for these missions.

89

DATE	ACTION
16-19Sep (Cont)	Cpl Summers again ventured out with the battalion scouts. After spending the night on hill 110 they spotted 4 VC who had an OP on a nearby hill. Cpl Summers called a mission in on them. He caused them to scatter but they didn't run fast enough and the fire for effect caught up with them. LCpl Boehme and LCpl Reid went with L Company to the area beyond hill 36. While there the platoon commander Lt. Squires and 3 men spotted about 50 VC. Lt Squires shot one of them as he was passing by. When the rest of the platoon arrived in the area the VC had hidden the body in the bushes. For some reason they also left the weapon. The VC fired at the platoon with automatic weapons while the platoon was retrieving the VC body. Maj Ruthauser, who was along with the patrol called for artillery in the area where the VC were. H&I fires were also plotted in that area. A boxing smoker was held at A/12. Competing for Btry "I" were Cpl Marlow, LCpl Huss, Pfc Mitchell, Pfc Taton and Pfc McClendon. Huss and Mitchell won their fights. While returning from a gravel run, Lt. Henderson picked up a sick Vietnamese and took him to Dong Da.

49

DATE	ACTION
22Sep-10ct	On Wednesday morning the battery was informed by a Marine Advisor that it would take part in an ARVN operation at Truoi Bridge and must be prepared to displace two guns by 1600. At that time the guns were escorted by an ARVN company to the operational area. The concept of the operation was for two ARVN units to form a pincer with the artillery to fire prep fires in the area between the pincers. As the pincers closed the prep fires would converge upon the central point so that the infantry would always have artillery fire in front of them. Lt. Cavagnol and Cpl Boehme were the FO's for the two ARVN units. The prep fires went as scheduled the nest morning. Also Lt. Cavagnol fired a number of on call will adjust missions. The operation destroyed a village and resulted in the capture of equipment and the detention of a number of suspects. At the end of the operation. Lt. Broesamle used Naval Gunfire to fire prearranged fires in the same area as the artillery had earlier.

An artillery operation was held in the area across the Song Ta Trach on Monday. Lt. Smith with the recon platoon set up an OP on hill 207; Lt. Henderson and Lt. Cavagnol were on 163 and Lt. Booth was on 153. Howtar battery was helelifted at 0600 to the base of hill 163 and Battery "I" displaced 4 guns to the Oasis. The artillery provided its own security and with the exception of recon, no infantry were used. Lt. Henderson made the first sighting of 3 VC in a house. He called in a destruction mission. When two of the adjusting rounds bracketed the building the 3 VC tried to sneak out. However, they didn't sneak well enough and Lt. Henderson called in a fire for effect which devastated the area. Lt. Smith made the next sighting at 1150 of 8 VC on a raft. He called in a mission and adjusted on them. The VC left the the raft and went into the underbrush. Lt. Smith then called in fire for effect using howtars and Battery "I". Nearly 200 rounds were fired. Lt. Smith then called for the reaction platoon from "I" Company to search the area for bodies. No bodies could be found but the reaction platoon leader, Lt. Downing reported that the area was so over grown that it would be possible to have 100 bodies there and never find one. The third sighting was made by Lts. Booth and Cavagnol on VC crossing the river. Lt Booth fired the mission because he had better visability. During the adjustment he observed about 24 VC crossing the river and an unknown number on each bank. He fired for effect several times getting excellent effect on the target area. The brush was to thick to see the bodies but at least 25% casualties could be estimated. Later in the afternoon LtCol Rudzis saw 3 VC near hill 153, Lt Henderson fired a mission on them with good effect on the target.

79.

DATE	ACTION

22Sep
1Oct
Cont

Battery "I" returned at about 1900 after having fired over 200
rounds during the operation. Lt Mullin's counterinsurgency
platoon made contact with about 15 VC in Phu Bai village at about
2200. The platoon was on patrol when the point man ran head-on
into a squad of VC. The two points ducked down and a fire fight
broke out when the rest of the platoon came up. The fight lasted
about 5 minutes and a Marine Cpl was killed, another man grazed
in the arm and a corpsman shot in the foot. The reaction platoon
was called out which included Cpl Marlatt and Cpl Deshano. By
this time the VC had broken contact but a search the next morning
revealed two VC bodies and weapons.

Lt. Cavagnol went on an ambush with "L" company to the Song Nang
near An Cu. Before they reached the ambush position the platoon
leader sent out six men to recon an area. One of the men saw a
VC coming out of the brush by a rice paddy. The VC turned to
fire but the cpl dropped to one knee and let go with his AR
killing the VC. At this time Lt. Cavagnol came up followed by
the rest of the platoon and joined in the shooting a VC was shot
and had a grenade thrown at him which exploded at his feet.
Another VC was firing from the brush but the heavy fire from the
platoon drove him off. Meanwhile Lt. Cavagnol had called in
illumination. When the illumination arrived it was nowhere near
on target and the rounds were going off on the ground. He called
for an end of mission and refired the mission with better effect.
The platoon commander would not allow him to use HE. A search
of the area at this time produced one VC body. The platoon spent
the night nearby and another search the next morning revealed
another VC body. There was also evidence that a third VC had
retreated in great haste. The battery received two 155mm
howitzers as has been expected due to the arrival of the self-
propelled 155's at battery "M". SSgt Woodard and Moulicp are
the section chiefs for these guns. It is noted that the battery
is now an eight gun battery. It is also noted that the battery
has had, at one time or another, every supporting weapon available
to the battalion except the 4.2 in mortar. That has included
tanks, ontos, 81mm mortars, 105's and 155's.

L-19's from the 220th aviation company have been experimenting
with aircraft flares as compared to the 155mm howitzer flare.
Also, it is being considered to put detection equipment in the
towers of the 220th's compound.

FLSU and K Company were probed by an estimated 8 VC. The
methods of April and May have not been forgotten. The number
of flares which lit up the entire perimeter and the ammunition
expended would have been worthy of a battalion.

79

DATE	ACTION

22Sep
1Oct
Cont

Lt. Broesamle and Pfc Fallucca went to Saigon to pick up a movie projector.

R&R continues to Bangkok and Okinawa with Lt's Beery and Schaeffer going to Bangkok and 1stSgt Satterfield to Okinawa. Hong Kong quotas are also expected again.

Meritorious Mast were presented to Cpl Marlatt and Cpl Gumto for outstanding performance of duty. These were presented by LtCol Rudzis at a battery formation.

The battery had a new surge of visitors during the week. Visiting were such notables as Col Calender, Reg CO; Col Part, Div G-1; LtCol Snyder, Reg S-3; Col Westrum and Maj Gen Van Ryzin.

LtCol Rudzis is planning to have more "artillery only" operations in the future such as the one described earlier. These are his own concept and pet project. This "artillery sniping" has already accounted for more damage to the VC than all the ambushes combined so it is undoubtadly worth the effort.

The following people have been evacuated for sickness:

Sgt Green   for malaria
Sgt Jones   for acute sinus trouble
Pfc Stack   ear trouble
Pfc Tracy   ear trouble

2 people have joined the battery and they are Pvt Johnson and LCpl Szebin.

Lt. Gustafson was out with a platoon from I Company near Highway #14 to set up an ambush when they heard an ARVN fire fight a few thousand meters from them. Illumination was fired by battery "M" in support of this fight as well as HE. The only problem was that the HE landed 200-300 meters behind Lt. Gustafson's position. This was disturbing to Lt. Gustafson for obvious reasons. It was also disturbing to the battalion FDC for equally obvious through different reasons. The upshot was that FDC asked Lt. Gustafson if he was certain that he wasn't getting incoming. Actually he was; it just wasn't VC incoming. A wire team was sniped at while repairing the wire to hill 225. They claimed to see the snipers go into a cave on Nui Mo Can and discovered that the "Cave" was in reality a large boulder.

A mess night was held in the Tuns Tavern Club. Guests included Capt Bao and 8 of his officers as well as the officers and staff NCO's of Battery "I". The menu included steaks (100 for 27 people) with baked potatoes and sour cream. There was red wine, white wine, Champaign, beer and cordials. Stewards were obtained from within the battery and silverware, china and glassware was scrounged from MAC V

DATE	ACTION

22Sep
1Oct
Cont

and 8th RRV. Cocktail hour began at 1800, dinner at about 1930 and most of the guests left at about 2230. However, the remainder of the guests stayed until about 0400. The cost was about $3.70 per man which just paid for beer (12 cases) The food was all donated (scrounged). Lt Henderson was the manager for the whole affair.

Capt. Harman fired in the defensive concentrations using shell smoke for ISU. Lt. Henderson was the FO and Maj Ritter was present. Five concentrations were fired encircleing ISU between the defensive perimeter and Loung Vam. Capt Harman also used this opportunity as a demonstration to point out artillery capabilities to Maj Ritter.

Capt Harman also went with LCpl Reed and Wilke to an nang to select positions for defensive concentrations. The selection of positions was made by the village chief under the advice of Sgt McCarthy who is the joint action squad leader for the village.

Cpl Lamb will join the joint action platoon in an nang as an FO. for about 30 days. Sgt Ellis will replace Cpl Lamb on Lt. Booth's FO team.

The district Hq near Hue was mortared and attached by a larger group of VC while attempting to fire an illumination round the fuze fell off and the round went off on the ground like a roman candle.

Jungle boots arrived at 3/4 and will be issued to FO teams.

2 Oct

LCpl Catoe with I Co was going out with an ambush to hill 36 and moved into position at about 2045. At about 2230 15 VC walked through the ambush. At least 2 VC were killed and their bodies recovered. 3 large sacks of rice were also found indicating the possibility of 4 more KIA's. An illumination mission was fired with HE under the illumination. The platoon then withdrew to a rallying point 400M south of the ambush site, and a defense was established. Another group of 10 VC were observed from this position and were fired upon Another sack of rice was found the next morning indicating another possible KIA.

An illumination grenade on the fence by CMR was found with its spoon tied. There was also evidence that somebody had been in the grass by the fence. Whoever the visitor was, he did not show up the next night.

LtCol Taylor has been relieved of 3/4 to take command of 3/9 . LtCol Vale is the new CO of 3/4.

91

DATE   ACTION

2Oct   Capt Harman, Lt. Henderson and Sgt Smith from battalion survey
              fired the concentrations in Phac Lan using shell smoke. The survey
              was not as good as Sgt McCardle use to do and the first round was
              way off. Lt Henderson then adjusted this round onto the target
              and called in the remaining missions as shifts from the first target.
              4 missions in all were fired.

              Lt. Smith with recon fired on about 15 VC across the river from
              hill 153 dispersing them.

82

India Battery Log, October 1965.

Transcribed from hand-written documents March 7, 2020.

The battery had a hootnanny on Sunday that featured a band plus four female and one male vocalist. It was held in the club. The troops, however, soon got into the show with Tateon on the drums and McAlpine on the guitar. Everyone else was on the bottle (or can). The music included rock and roll, popular and country and western. At times the Vietnamese could hardly be understood which is okay because the words weren't meant to be understood and most everybody was too drunk to listen anyway. However, they were not too drunk to fire a mission a little later on. The cost of the affair was $30.

In FO action, Lt. Booth set up an OP on hill 207 when howtar battery displaced to hill 163 but didn't see any VC. Lt. Gustafson set up an OP on hill 139 and fired a number of concentrations while Lt. Cavagnol went into Phu Bai village, getting very wet but seeing no VC.

LtCol Vale, the new CO *(Oct 1 1965)* for 3/4 toured Battery "I" and was satisfied with the position. He was particularly impressed by the galley and by CMR.

An increase of VD which has had its origins in the Hong Kong Bar has brought an end to prostitution in that establishment. 6 girls will be retained as waitresses. Virtue wins again.

General Krulak paid a visit to Phu Bai again but did not tour the area, nor did he bring any new information concerning the status of the battalion.

Senator Brewster of Maryland visited Phu Bai also *(Oct 12, 1965)*. He stopped by 3/4, 4/12, HMM 161, and 8th RRU as well as Battery I. He also toured the TAOR by helicopter where he was supposed to stop on 225 but did not because of bad weather. The Senator was in a Marine Raider battalion during WW II and impressed everybody he met.

The battery underwent a division ordinance inspection conducted by LtCol Ragsdale who has been in the Marine Corps for 30 years. He found many sea stories to tell of the old corps. He also found every unit he inspected, including Battery "I" to be "unsat". He seemed not pleased with the 3.5's and machine guns (that is if "horrible" can be considered a term of displeasure). He also found carbon in the 105 chambers, lack of bore cleaner and rags not constituting a valid excuse with him. He did say that Battery "I" had the best laid out position he had ever seen. Therefore, it would seem that Battery "I" is the best "unsat" battery in the Marine Corps.

Recon set up a daylight OP by hill 53 (*Oct. 10, Hill 52, Coord 814125)* and spotted 3 VC coming their way. Recon took cover, let the VC get close and opened fire, killing one and wounding one. Then the rest of the recon company was called out and one of the helicopters was fired on. Therefore, the reaction platoon from K company was also called out and swept the area finding no more VC. The wounded VC was taken to A med and has been talking ever since.

Major Watson (*executive officer, should be Webster*) left 4/12 (*Oct. 15)* to be replaced by Major Speisel . Capt. Harmon and 1st Sgt Satterfield saw Major Webster off.

Lt. Gustafson set up an OP on hill 50 and fired saturation fires on the 9005 grid square while K company set up a blocking force. It was believed that there was a company of VC in the area and the artillery would drive them into the blocking force. It didn't work.

1st Lt. William P. Shaeffer relieves Capt. Donnie N. Harman as CO of Battery "I" on 15 Oct 1965

HEADQUARTERS
3d Battalion, 4th Marines(Rein)
1st Marine Brigade, FMF
c/o FPO, San Francisco 96601

3/FSR/jwd
28 April 65

From: Commanding Officer
To: Commanding General, 9th Marine Expeditionary Brigade
Via: Commanding Officer, Regimental Landing Team 3

Subj: After Action Report

Ref: (a) Telcon with Crowd-3 26 April 1965
       (b) 9th MEB Lot Ser 0024-65 dtd 20 April 1965

1. In accordance with verbal instructions (reference (a)) and written instructions (reference (b)) the following after action report is submitted.

2. After Action Report:

    a. Statistical data:

        (1) Unit, 2nd Squad, 3d Platoon, Company B, 3d Reconnaissance Battalion, 4th Marines (Rein), 1st Marine Brigade, FMF.

        (2) Strength: Ten (10) Marine Enlisted; one (1) Navy enlisted.

        (3) Time of departure: 241200H April 1965.

        (4) Time of return: 251100H April 1965.

        (5) Nature of Operation: Area reconnaissance.

        (6) Area location: An Nong W sheet 125 34 W 1:25,000; area bound by coordinates; 878094, 897095, 897087, 868082, 864089.

        (7) Time of contact: 250107H April 1965.

        (8) Location of contact: Coordinates 861084.

        (9) Enemy disposition after contact: Two (2) KIA, one (1) probable WIA.

        (10) Friendly disposition after contact: Two (2) KIA, four (4) WIA.

        (11) Equipment: Two (2) enemy automatic wpns captured, three (3) gernades captured. No friendly equipment lost.

90

b. Narrative account of action: The patrol left the friendly position at 1200 and arrived in the assigned area approximately 1200. At approximately 1730 it was reported there was an enemy battalion moving to the south west of the patrol area. The patrol was directed to move to the high ground to observe this target. The patrol moved to coordinates 865076 but did not make visual contact with the enemy battalion. After night fall approximately 2000 the patrol was directed to move to hill 144 coordinates 865096. The patrol leader moved to what he believed was hill 144 but in fact he was located at coordinates 861084. Approximately 2200 the patrol leader requested to send a team to reconoiter his front. This request was denied. The patrol leader then sent two men to his rear (southwest) to bobby trap a trail leading to his position. These two men were to return by 2400. Small arms fire was heard in the vincinity of the two men between 2330 and 0100. At 0107 a Viet Cong patrol of five to nine men jumped the position of the patrol, approaching up a very steep slope to the rear (west) of the patrol. The enemy patrol was within twenty meters of the center of the friendly patrol and opened up with automatic weapons. The friendly patrol returned fire killing two of the VC and wounding one. The remainder of the patrol moved down the slope.

At 0200 1stLt REASONER, Plat Comdr of the reconnisance platoon left the battalion area with the first squad of the reconnaissance platton and moved to hill 144 the alleged location of the second squad. When he did not find the second squad on hill 144 he requested the squad fire a red flare to disclose their position. Sighting the flare he then moved to hill 161 and organized a defense of the hill and requested air evacuation for the wounded. This request was denied until daylight. At 0610 the helicopter arrived and landed without incident and carried away one dead Marine, one dead VC and three wounded Marines. Lt REASONER then searched for th two missing Marines finding one alive but wounded at coordinates 866084 and then found the other Marine dead at coordinates 860081. Air evacuation was requested and arrived at approximately 0800. The platoon commander and the squad leader returned to battalion CP and were debriefed by the Battalion Commanding Officer.

c. Lessons learned: The Viet Cong are very stealthy and patient and are not to be underestimated. They can move difficult terrain.

d. Difficulties encountered: Navigation during the hours of darkness is very difficult in this terrain due to the fact that all the high ground is shaped similar.

e. Training: The patrols must live in the area and get to know the terrain as well as the enemy knows it before they can fight on equal terms with the VC.

91

f. Suggestions for future operations: The reconnaissance platoon live in the TAOR and depend on serial and surface resupply. Work the assigned area continuously until each man is very familiar with the terrain and then observe all movement of the VC within the area and through the use of timely and ddfinate reporting alert the infantry units so that the enemy patrols can be ambushed.

                              JAMES S. CONRADO Jr.
                              By direction

92

HEADQUARTERS
3d Battalion, 4th Marines
1st Marine Brigade, FMF
c/o FPO, San Francisco 96601

3/JSC/jwd
14 May 1965

From: Commanding Officer
To: Commanding General, 9th Marine Expiditionary Brigade
Via: Commanding Officer, Regimental Landing Team 3

Subj: After Action Report #2

Ref: (a)   Telcon with Crowd-3 26 April 1965
        (b)   9th MEB Lot Ser 0024-65 dtd 20 April 1965

1.   In accordance with verbal instructions (reference (a)) and written
instructions (reference (b)) the following after action report is submitted.

2.   After Action Report:
     a.
     a.   Statiscal data:

         (1)   Units involved:

                (a)   3d Platoon, Company B, 3d Reconnaissance Battalion,
4th Marines (Rein), 1st Marine Brigade, FMF.

                (b)   2nd Platoon, Company M, 3d Battalion,14th Marines (Rein),
1st Marine Brigade, FMF.

                (c)   3d Platoon, Company L, 3d Battalion, 4th Marines (rein),
1st Marine Brigade, FMF.

                (d)   Battery "I", 3d Battalion, 12th Marines, 1st Marine Brigade,
FMF.

                (e)   Detachment, Avn Company, 1st ARVN Adv

                (f)   Two armed UH-1's.

                (g)   One L-19.

         (2)   Time commenced: 130600H May 1965.

         (3)   Time ended: 131800H May 1965.

         (4)   Nature of operation: Reconnaissance in force.

         (5)   Initial objective: Hill 163,at YD. 812079.

93

b. Narrative account of action: Suntan 6 initiated a reconnaissance in force consisting of 3d Platoon, Company B 3d Reconnaissance Battalion (-), the second platoon of Company M the third platoon of Company L, India Battery, two armed UH-1B's; and on L-19. India Battery displaced to YD 868118 to support the mission.

At 0600 Recon moved off hill 225 YD 848086. BM/2 started for hill 101 YD 828086 keeping to the higher ground and acting as a diversionary force. L/3 moved into position on hill 97 YD 841082 at 0812. Recon spotted a VC patrol of 8-10 men. Recon called artillery fire on the VC patrol and they dispersed. Recon coordinated with M/2 and hunted the dispersed VC. The searched netted a still warm cooking pot with rice, an MAS 36, 7.62mm rifle, a pair of sandals and a supply of rice. This information was relayed to Suntan 6 on Hill225, and Suntan 6 directed both Recon and M/2 to proceed to Hill 163. L/3 was ordered to move to hill 101.

When Recon and M/2 arrived on Hill 163, M/2 secured the hill and Recon proceeded to the villiage located at YD 8007. Squad from M/2 swept the draws on the flanks of Hill 163 with no results.

Upon arrival in the villiage area, Recon found framed thatched houses, obviously lived in, warm food , caves fighting holes, cultivated land and a large coche of rice. About this time the platoon commander began hearing noises in the bush . He set his men in a 360 degree perimeter and put one team into an ambush. One VC walked into the ambush. His comrades called to him from the brush, but as he turned and ran, three shots from Recon ambush ripped into him. The ambush team left him lie while trying to intize his comrades to come for him. .When this proved futile, they recovered the VC, patched his wound, moved him out of the villiage to an LZ and evacuated him by helo to B-Med at Phu Bai Airfield. Recon then retired from the villiageand returned to the base of hill 163 where platoon commanders was directed to report to hill225. After Recon retired, artillery fire was called and the villiage area was shelled with HE fuze delay and WP. During Recon's return to hill 225 a lone VC was sighted. Lt. REASONER took one team and actually ran the man down. He was seen to throw his rifle into a stream. Interrogation later confimmed this fact. The captured VC was returned by helo to base camp. Both prisoners were part of the original squad sighted earlier in the day.

In the mean while, M/2 on Hill 163 sent a reinforced squad to the villiage. This squad's report parralleled recon's report. The patrol reported large cultivated areas of fruit, bananas, pineapples and vege-tables which the patrol destroyed, in part. Thevilliage was deserted with no indications of women or children living there. There were bloodstains on several of the trails leaving the villiage in a southermly direction.

M/2 was directed to remain on Hill 163 for the night. L/3 was directed to remain on Hill 101, Company L (-) was dispatched to Hill 97 prepatory to a sweep of the villiage area beginning 140600H May 1965.

An intelligence brief will follow under seperate correspondence.

The operation was supported by the armed UHB's until mid-afternoon. India Battery fired 159 rounds in support of the mission.

94

c. Results of operations:

1 VC wounded - later died.
1 VC captured.
2 VC rifles, MAS 36, 7.62mm.
600 lbx. of rice.
3 cane knivies.
25 rounds of 7.62mm ammo.
1 ammo pouch and belt and U.S. poncho.
13 Flashlight batteries.
2.packs of candy.
Assorted cooking utensiles and rice bowls.
1 pair sandals.
3 pair trousers.
Assorted clothing.
1 flash light.

JAMES S. CONRADO, Jr.
By direction

95

Kim Le Bat, Thuy Phu Village chief, points out one of his 11 surveyed artillery concentration areas to Maj. Gen. Lewis W. Walt, commander of the 3d Marine Amphibious Force. Lt. Col. W. W. Taylor (left) commanding the 3d Bn., 4th Marine Regt., and assistant village chief Vang help explain the area and purpose of the surveyed fields of fire. (USMC)

Leatherneck Artillery Serves Twofold Purpose in Vietnam

By WO JIM SMITH

HUE-PHU BAI, Vietnam (ISO) —A Marine artillery battery has found a solution for stopping Viet Cong attacks and has shown the Vietnamese tangible evidence marines are here to help defend against communist aggression.

The plan began April 16 when Capt. D. N. Harman of Coppers Cove, Tex., landed in the Republic of Vietnam as commanding officer of I Btry., 3d Bn., 12th Marine Regt. The battery is attached to the 3d Bn., 4th Marine Regt., which provides defense for the Hue-Phu Bai airfield complex.

The plan was simply to destroy the Viet Cong, who then controlled many of the surrounding villages, by surveying artillery concentrations on all possible avenues of enemy access to the villages—with the consent of the local people.

Several village chiefs met with Harman to hear his proposal and to witness the accuracy and effectiveness of an artillery bombardment. The chiefs were evacuated.

"Our surveyed fields of fire are a defensive artillery plan," reported Harman. The captain, who was a marine private in the artillery during the Korean War, added, "It also serves to protect the Vietnamese people, and to immediately counter any Viet Cong attack against the airfield defenses."

A surveyed concentration requires perfection and precision by every member of the artillery team. There has not been a death or injury to the local Vietnamese people since the artillery began firing the concentration system.

"The surveyed concentration target areas have a definite deterrent effect against the enemy, and have greatly increased the relations which our marines enjoy with the Vietnamese people in our combined fight against the Viet Cong," said Maj. Gen. Lewis W. Walt, commanding general of the 3d Marine Amphibious Force.

Thirteen hamlets are now protected by the Marine-surveyed artillery plan.

Sgt. T. L. McCaudle of Richton, Miss., survey chief for "I" Battery, walked more than 200 miles while surveying each concentration area.

He was assisted by three other artillery men and, normally, a squad of infantry from the 3d Bn., 4th Marine Regt.

More than 7,000 rounds of artillery projectiles have been fired into the surveyed concentrations to date from the six 105mm howitzers.

Thus far, three Viet Cong attacks have been stopped by the pin-point accuracy. There has never been an actual body count of dead Viet Cong, because the enemy quickly removes his dead.

MILITARY ASSISTANCE COMMAND, VIETNAM, INFORMATION OFFICE

COMBAT INFORMATION BUREAU
III MARINE AMPHIBIOUS FORCE
FLEET MARINE FORCE
FPO, SAN FRANCISCO, 96601

Release No: 353-65
By: WO Jim Smith

artillery

Bach Dang Street
Da Nang, Vietnam
Tel: Motley 41

FOR IMMEDIATE RELEASE:

HUE/PHU BAI, Vietnam, Aug. 3 — A Marine artillery battery has found a solution for stopping Viet Cong attacks and, simultaneously, has shown the Vietnamese tangible evidence that Marines are here to help in the defense against communist aggression.

The plan began April 16 when Marine Capt. D. N. Harman of Coppers Cove, Tex., landed in Vietnam as commanding officer of "I" Battery, 3rd Bn., Twelfth Marine Regiment. The battery is attached to the 3rd Bn., Fourth Marine Regiment, which provides defense for the Hue/Phu Bai airfield complex.

The plan was simple. Destroy the Viet Cong, which then controlled many of the surrounding villages, by surveying artillery concentrations on all possible avenues of enemy access to the villages; and get the consent of the local people.

Several village chiefs met with Capt. Harman to hear his proposal and to witness the accuracy and effectiveness of an artillery bombardment. The chiefs were so impressed with the destructive power of artillery that on June 20 three of five villages, with more than 15,000 population, consented to the captain's plan.

-more-

Each artillery concentration area is surveyed, the distance walked, checked and rechecked, and smoke is fired to pin-point the target. Final corrections are made on the guns, and "fire for effect" can be initiated by the village chiefs at any given moment.

The plan is perfected in such detail that only seconds elapse from the time the request is received until the first 33-pound projectile is hurled into the target area.

Each firing mission is called for by the village chiefs, but only after all the people have been evacuated.

"Our surveyed fields of fire are a defensive artillery plan," reported Capt. Harman. The captain, a Marine private in artillery during the Korean War, added, "It also serves to protect the Vietnamese people, and to immediately counter any Viet Cong attack against the airfield defenses."

A surveyed concentration requires perfection and precision by every member of the artillery team. There has never been a death or injury to the local Vietnamese people since the artillery commenced firing the concentration system.

"The surveyed concentration target areas have a definite deterrent effect against the enemy, and have greatly increased the relations which our Marines enjoy with the Vietnamese people in our combined fight against the Viet Cong," stated MajGen. Lewis W. Walt, commanding general of the III Marine Amphibious Force.

Kim Le Bat, village chief for Thuy Phu, was the first chief to request the artillery survey of his five hamlets for a concentration fire area. The concentration was named in his honor.

-more-

artillery —3-3-3-3-3-3-3-3

Thirty-two other concentrations bear the names of village officials, or of important people from within the village complex of hamlets.

Thuy Phu, with 11 concentrations, was followed quickly by the village chiefs of Phuy Tan with eight, Thuy Luong with 14, and, recently Thuy An Nonj. Thuy An Nonj became a member of the "club" July 28; five concentrations have already been listed for the village.

Thirteen hamlets are now protected by the Marine-surveyed artillery plan.

Sgt. T. L. McCaudle of Richton, Miss., survey chief for "I" Battery, walked more than 200 miles while surveying each concentration area.

He was assisted by three other artillery men and, normally, a squad of infantry from the 3rd Bn., Fourth Marine Regiment. The squad was a protective measure against Viet Cong attacks while surveying the concentrations.

More than 7,000 rounds of artillery projectiles have been fired into the surveyed concentrations to date from the six 105mm howitzers.

Thus far, three Viet Cong attacks have been stopped by the pin-point accuracy. There has never been an actual body count of dead Viet Cong, however; the enemy quickly removes his dead to eliminate possible intelligence information falling into Marine hands.

—usmc—

Pinpoint Artillery Fire Stops Viet Cong Attack, Aids Friendly Villagers

HUE/PHU BAI, Vietnam,-- A Marine artillery battery has found a solution for stopping Viet Cong attacks and, simultaneously, has shown the Vietnamese tangible evidence that Marines are here to help in the defense against communist aggression.

The plan began April 16 when Marine Captain D.N. Harman, landed in Vietnam as commanding officer of "I" Battery, 3rd Bn., Twelfth Marine Regiment. The battery is attached to the 3rd Bn., Fourth Marine Regiment, which provides defense for the Hue/Phu Bai airfield complex.

The plan was simple. Destroy the Viet Cong which then controlled many of the surrounding villages, by surveying artillery concentrations on all possible avenues of enemy access to the villages, and get the consent of the local people.

Several village chiefs met with Capt. Harman to hear his proposal and to witness the accuracy and effectiveness of an artillery bombardment. The chiefs were so impressed with the destructive power of artillery that on June 20 three of five villages, with more than 15,000 population, consented to the captain's plan.

Each artillery concentration area is surveyed, the distance walked, checked and rechecked, and smoke is fired to pinpoint the target. Final corrections are made on the guns, and "fire for effect" can be initiated by the village chiefs at any given moment.

The plan is perfected in such detail that only seconds elapse from the time the request is received until the first 33-pound projectile is hurled into the target area.

Each firing mission is called for by the village chiefs, but only after all the people have been evacuated.

"Our surveyed fields of fire are a defensive artillery plan," reported Capt. Harman. The captain, a Marine private in artillery during the Korean War, added, "It also serves to protect the Vietnamese people, and to immediately counter any Viet Cong attack against the airfield defenses."

A surveyed concentration requires perfection and precision by every member of the artillery team. There has never been a death or injury to the local Vietnamese people since the artillery commenced firing the concentration system.

"The survey concentration target areas have a definite deterrent effect against the enemy, and have greatly increased the relations which our Marines enjoy with the Vietnamese people in our combined fight against the Viet Cong," stated Major General Lewis W. Walt, commanding general of the III Marine Amphibious Force.

Kim Le Bat, village chief for Thuy Phu, was the first chief to request the artillery survey of his five hamlets for a concentration fire area. The concentration was named in his honor.

Thuy Phu, with 11 concentrations, was followed quickly by the village chiefs of Phuy Tan with eight, Thuy Luong with 14, and, recently Thuy An Nonj. Thuy An Nonj became a member of the "club" July 28; five concentrations have already been listed for the village.

Thirteen hamlets are now protected by the Marine-surveyed artillery plan.

Sergeant T. L. McCandle, survey chief for "I" Battery, walked more than 200 miles while surveying each concentration area.

He was assisted by three other artillery men and, normally, a squad of infantry from the 3rd Bn., Fourth Marine Regiment. The squad was a protective measure against Viet Cong attacks while surveying the concentrations.

More than 7,000 rounds of artillery projectiles have been fired into the surveyed concentrations to date from the six 105mm howitzers.

Thus far, three Viet Cong attacks have been stopped by the pin-point accuracy. There has never been an actual body count of dead Viet Cong, however; the enemy quickly removes his dead to eliminate possible intelligence information falling into Marine hands.

Transcribed from hand written documents March 7, 2020

Actions Dealing with Pre-Planned Fires in Villages

23 June 65: Met with three village chiefs at Artillery CP to discuss capabilities of artillery and firing of concentrations. Stressed the method of surveying in targets, marking the area of concentration with smoke to avoid hurting anyone. Chiefs very receptive…served cold apple juice which was enjoyed by all.

24 June: Picked up village chiefs at Thuy Tan and Thuy Luong and went to Phu Bai to fire in smoke concentrations, very effective. Chiefs' impressed by firing of concentrations. A name system was established for concentrations rather than the normal numbering. Each chief will name his concentrations after key village members. Chiefs' were impressed with this. Survey team with infantry squad has been in Thuy Phu for three days putting in survey. Villagers very receptive, and particularly impressed with theodolite and aiming circle.

25 to 29 June: Survey team with ARVN Artillery survey team went to Thuy Tan and Thu Luong to establish survey control. Security provided by infantry squad. Very good reception by people.

2 July: General Krulak went to Thuy Phu and observed smoke rounds fired on concentrations. Le Bat impressed over visits of Krulak and being able to show him his maps with named concentrations. Krulak autographed maps and had tea with Le Bat.

3 July: Capt. Harman, Lt. Henderson, survey party and security squad to Thuy Phu. Placed two more concentrations. Le Bat informed Capt. Harman of a VC assembly and supply area. Capt. Harmon gave Lt. Col. Taylor an intelligence briefing on the Thuy Phu area. Particularly in regards to the information received from Le Bat concerning VC activities in woodland area. Col. Taylor planning operation there as a result.

5 July: Capt. Harman and Lt. Henderson made brief call upon Le Bat.

6 July: Capt. Harman, Lt. Henderson, and Sgt. McCardle to Thuy Luong. Met with village chief, Pham Hy, discussed placing concentrations around his village. Emphasis was placed on Pham Hy picking out concentrations where he wanted them, and naming them after his own people. Chief impressed over this arrangement and very receptive to Marines extending their services. General areas for concentrations decided upon. Final decision to be made next day.

7 July: Lt. Henderson, Lt. Dau (ARVN), Sgt. McCardle and infantry squad to Thuy Luong. Met with Pham Hy and walked the terrain, picking out five concentrations to be named, Phan Thi, Vo Chau, Nguyen Nhan, Phan Thi, and Bach Ngot. Chief very eager to have concentrations around his village. Marines distributed candy and cigarettes to villagers. Survey party completed surveying in concentrations.

8 July: Capt. Harman, Lt. Henderson, Sgt. McCardle and ARVN interpreter to Thuy Tan. Chief Le Dinh Sad was not present. Capt. Harman pointed out 3 concentrations to be surveyed in around Thuy Tan. Survey completed that afternoon. Capt. Bao sent two tape men to help with survey. One

squad of Marines sent as security for survey party; upon arrival in village, Popular Force platoon commander gave party 6 P.F. troops as security. Lt. Henderson then secured Marine squad and sent them back to base camp. Villagers extremely receptive to Marine survey party; especially fascinated by aiming circle and binoculars.

9 July: Capt. Harman, Lt. Henderson and Sgt. McCardle to Thuy Luong; picked up Pham Hy and went to concentration area. Capt. Harman shot in and adjusted concentrations. Excellent data from survey. Slight problem encountered keeping villagers and Marine Recon squad out of impact area. Pham Hy pleased with concentrations; brought party back to his headquarters for beer. 0930 arrived Thuy Tan and took Chief Le Dinh Sad out to observe concentrations. Capt Harman again adjusted fires, brought concentration within 100 meters of party. This concentration was fired one hour later for General Karch and Col. Wheeler who came to Thuy Tan to observe effects of the artillery "people to people" program.

14 July: Sgt McCardle, Squad Security (I Co) Lt. Dau (ARVN Art.) Capt Harman and Kim Le Bat to Phu Bai complex to fire in concentrations: Harman, Le, Chau, Ap Hi, Sung, Bang, Bat, Vang. Kim Le next served tea and Beetle nuts. Informed me 7 V.C. were in the village Phu Bai 11 July. He desires a helicopter ride. He gave Capt. Harman a dog but the Captain stated he would wait until after his helicopter ride. He has the picture of General Krulak on his desk and is quite impressed; along with ….a …from the concentration….

18 July: Maj. Baity, Capt. Harman, Lt. Henderson, Sgt. McCardle, and security squad to Thuy Luong and Thu Tan. Registered Howtar Battery in Thuy Luong on concentration Thi. First round landed 40 meters from registration point---about 200 meters from OP. Precision registration conducted…two target hits. At completion of Howtar registration, India Battery fired smoke check rounds on all five Thuy Luong concentrations; all rounds hit within 20 meters of surveyed points; excellent data. Drove to Thuy Tan and picked up village chief Le Dinh Sad, and five of his men. Battery "I" fired smoke check rounds on Sinh, Quan, and Do; adjusted Quan, and Do; adjusted Quan and Do for Le Dinh Sad.

1 Aug 1965: Major Baity, Capt. Harman, Lt. Weld and the survey section went to the village of An Nong. After making liaison with the village chief we toured the village area with the chief to determine the location of artillery concentrations to support the defense of the village. The survey section took note of the locations that the village chief indicated the V.C. operated in and began to put in survey control data.

2 Aug: Major Webster, Maj. Baity, Capt Harmon shot concentrations A, B, C, D, & E at Thuy An Nong.

survey control. Security provided by infantry squad. Very good reception by people.

2 JULY — General Krulak went to Thuy Phu and observed smoke rounds fired on concentrations. Lt Batt impressed over visit of Krulak and being able to show him his map with named concentrations. Krulak autographed maps and had tea with Lt Sat.

3 JULY — Capt. Harman, Lt. Henderson, survey party and security squad to Thuy Phu. Placed two more concentrations. Le Bat informed Capt. Harman of a VC assembly and supply area. Capt. Harman gave Lt Col Taylor an intelligence briefing on the Thuy Phu area particularly in regard to the information received from Le Bat concerning VC activities in woodland area. Col Taylor planning operation there as a result.

5 July — Capt Harman and Lt. Henderson made first call upon Le Sat.

6 July — Capt. Harman, Lt. Henderson, and Sgt. McArdle to Thuy Luong. Mets with village chief, Pham Hy, discussed placing concentrations around his

There were seven pages of handwriting in the above transcript. Whose handwriting is this?

DID PRE-PLANNED FIRES FOR VIETNAMESE VILLAGE CHIEFS WORK?

This entry found in the S-3 Journal Section of the **3rd Battalion 4th Marines Command Chronology** for 27 July 1965:

2145: Village Chief THUY PHU "Request fire mission at coord. 905099, 909102, and 913106 VC moving into area. Mission approved and fired 2 HE apiece."

India Battery was about 6000 meters away or about 3.7 miles. What was the dispersion pattern of the incoming high explosive shells?

This seems like a crazy idea. Let untrained Vietnamese Village chiefs call in artillery fire and risk civilian casualties. But it looks like it worked. Who thought of the idea? Captain Harman received a Bronze Star for this.

Who thought of: (1) Pre-planned fires for the Vietnamese village chiefs and (2) firing in a 6400 mil circle (360 degrees) ? I never heard of any other battery doing that either in Vietnam or later in my years in the Marine Reserve.

In the name of the President of the United States, the Commanding General, Fleet Marine Force, Pacific takes pleasure in presenting the BRONZE STAR MEDAL to

CAPTAIN DONNIE NEWT HARMAN

UNITED STATES MARINE CORPS

for service as set forth in the following

CITATION:

"For meritorious achievement in connection with operations against the enemy while serving as Commanding Officer of Battery I, 3d Battalion, 12th Marines in the Republic of Vietnam from 14 April 1965 to 8 July 1965. An extremely capable and resourceful leader, Captain HARMAN won the confidence of his superiors and served as an inspiration to his subordinates through his diligence and devotion to duty. Through his foresight in preparing his battery for any tactical situation, a state of combat readiness far greater than normally expected of an artillery battery was achieved. Demonstrating his professional skill as an artillery officer, he provided the 3d Battalion, 4th Marines with immediate, continuous and extremely accurate artillery support. Attaining an outstanding degree of coordination with the Army of the Republic of Vietnam, Captain HARMAN materially contributed to the total military effort in the Hue-Phu-Bai area. On his own initiative, he coordinated with the village chiefs in the Phu Bai area in the planning for and firing of pre-registered artillery concentrations in defense of their villages. Through, his skill and judicious use of tact and diplomacy when dealing with village chiefs, Captain HARMAN inspired confidence and cooperation between the local populace and the American military personnel. Concerned for the welfare of his men, he provided his unit with living accommodations and recreation facilities far higher than normally thought possible under field conditions. Captain HARMAN's leadership, initiative and devotion to duty were in keeping with the highest traditions of the United States Naval Service."

Captain HARMAN is authorized to wear the Combat "V".

FOR THE PRESIDENT

A. R. KIER
MAJOR GENERAL, U. S. MARINE CORPS
ACTING COMMANDING GENERAL

TEMPORARY CITATION

JOURNAL
NAVMC 219-63 (REV. 8-56)
SUPERSEDES PREVIOUS EDITION
WHICH MAY BE USED

UNIT OR STAFF SECTION
TI-8

ORGANIZATION
BATTERY "I" -3-12

OPENED (DTG, Month, year)
11 1900 MAY

CLOSED (DTG, Month, year)
25 1200 MAY

(Classification)

TIME		SER. NO.	DTG	INCIDENTS, MESSAGES, ORDERS, ETC.	ACTION TAKEN M-Maps T-Troops S-Staff F-File
IN	OUT				
			11 1900 H	LT. HENDERSON + CPL. MARLATT arrived OP Virginia (Hill 180)	
			11 2030 H	ROUTINE CALL FROM CAPT. HARMAN	
			11 2330 H	SUSPECTED ENEMY PROBE. GRENADE THROWN, 8 SHOTS FIRED; AREA ILLUMINATED, NO CASUALTIES	CALLED TI-22 TO REPORT INCIDENT.
			11 2345 H	LT. COL. TAYLOR CALLED FOR DETAILS OF INCIDENT.	
			12 0730 H	SGT. FEATHERSTON CALLED REGARDS SUPPLY. REQUESTED MAP # 125 33, MAP BOARD + ACETATE, CP & GP TENTS.	
			12 0830 H	REQUESTED TO FIRE CONCENTRATION AT COORD. 807106 NEGATIVE PERMISSION... OUT OF FREE ZONE	
			12 1230 H	REQUESTED TO FIRE CONCENTRATION AT 802 093 — NEGATIVE PERMISSION... ARUN TERRITORY.	
			12 1400 H	NON-TACTICAL PARA-DROP IN GRID SQUARE 8812.	RELAYED INFO TO TI-3 + TI-4
			12 2030 H	FIREFIGHT BY PHUBAI VILLAGE AZIMUTH 1825.	REPORTED TO TI 22
			12 2110 H	GUNFIRE + ILLUMINATION BY HUE RADIO STATION 12 6091	REPORTED TO TI 22
			13 0005 H	GUNFIRE ON HILL 225	REPORTED TO TI 22
			13 1300 H	106 SQUAD REPLACED BY NEW SQUAD. FLY TENT ERECTED	
			13 1530 H	4 UNIDENTIFIED TROOPS SPOTTED AT COORDINATES 805095 AZ 4145. LOST SIGHT OF THEM BEHIND RIDGE LINE.	REPORTED TO TI-22. TOLD TO DISREGARD
			13 1700 H	CALLED S-4 FOR SUPPLY; REQUESTED SANDBAGS, BORE CLEANER, 50 CAL BORE BRUSH, WATER, LUMBER, LYE, GP TENT, FLARES	

PAGE NO: (Classification)

117

UNIT OR STAFF SECTION
TI-8

ORGANIZATION
BATTERY "I"-3-12

OPENED (DTG, Month, year)	CLOSED (DTG, Month, year)
11 1900 MAY	25 1200 MAY

(Classification)

TIME		SER. NO.	DTG	INCIDENTS, MESSAGES, ORDERS, ETC.	ACTION TAKEN M-Maps T-Troops S-Staff F-File
IN	OUT				
			13 2030 H	SPOTTED CONTINUOUS ILLUMINATION (4 ROUNDS) IN VICINITY OF HUE, AZ 5115.	REPORTED TO TI 22
			14 0100 H	RELAYED SIT. REPORT TO TI FOR TI-4A.	
			14 1300 H	RESUPPLIED WITH C-RATIONS + WATER BY HELICOPTER.	
			14 1500 H	OBSERVED TANKS CLOSING IN ON VC COORDINATES 819155 AZ 5210	KEPT TI-22 INFORMED ON SITUATION
			14 1630 H	SPOTTED 1 PERSON WALKING AROUND VICINITY OF TANK ACTION AT COORDINATES 819155	REPORTED TO TI-22 WHO CONTACTED ARUN
			14 1800 H	HELICOPTER FLEW IN 4 MAN REACTIONARY FORCE FROM B-MED.	
			14 1900 H	RECEIVED STONEWALL REPORT FROM TI-4A	RELAYED TO TI 22
			14 2015 H	SPOTTED SMALL FIRE AT AZ 4520, APPROX. 8000 METERS	REPORTED TO TI-22
			14 2130 H	SPOTTED SMALL FIRE AT AZ 4745, APPROX 8000 METERS	REPORTED TO TI-22
			15 0630 H	REACTION FORCE LEFT HILL ON FOOT.	
			15 0730 H	CALLED CAPT. FRY REGARDS DELAY IN RECEIVING GP TENT, SANDBAGS, + FLARES.	
			15 1430 H	HELICOPTER SUPPLY RUN: RECEIVED GP TENT, SANDBAGS, FLARES.	
			15 1800 H	HELICOPTER FLEW IN 4 MAN REACTIONARY FORCE.	

PAGE NO: (Classification)

(Classification)

UNIT OR STAFF SECTION	
TI-8	
ORGANIZATION	
BATTERY "I" - 3 - 12	
OPENED (DTG, Month, year)	CLOSED (DTG, Month, year)
11 1900 MAY	25 1200 MAY

TIME		SER.	DTG	INCIDENTS, MESSAGES, ORDERS, ETC.	ACTION TAKEN
IN	OUT	NO.			M-Maps T-Troops S-Staff F-File
			15 2345 H	SPOTTED FLARE AZ 1747 APPROX. 4000 METERS.	REPORTED TO TI-22
			16 0300 H	DITTO	DITTO
			16 0630 H	REACTION FORCE LEFT AREA.	
			17 0730 H	NEW TRASH PIT BLOWN BY ENGINEERS	
			17 0800 H	GP TENT ERECTED, SAND BAGS FILLED & PLACED AROUND TENTS, MACHINE GUN, 106's, & AMMO PIT.	
			17 1300 H	TEST FIRED 106's, M-60, & INDIVIDUAL WEAPONS.	
			17 2030 H	OBSERVED CONTINUOUS ILLUMINATION NEAR PHU BAI VILLAGE, AZ 2040	REPORTED TO TI-22
			18 0200 H	OBSERVED INTENSIVE FIRE FIGHT NEAR RADIO STATION, AZ 6020	
			19 0215 H	ADVISED M-3 THAT VC MIGHT RETROGRADE FROM RADIO STATION THROUGH THEIR AREA.	REPORTED TO TI-22
			18 0630 H	REACTION FORCE LEFT AREA.	
			18 0700 H	COL. WHEELER & LT. COL. TAYLOR INSPECTED AREA PRIOR TO KRULAK'S VISIT. WELL PLEASED WITH AREA.	
			18 0830 H	CAPT. SEEBURGER ARRIVED IN AREA. BRIEFED ON HILL 180 MISSION & OPERATION.	
			18 0945 H	GEN. KRULAK, CG FMF PAC, ARRIVED HILL 180. SATISFIED WITH ORGANIZATION, BUT THOUGHT BARBED WIRE WAS TOO CLOSE TO POSITIONS.	
			18 1300 H	HELICOPTER SUPPLY RUN.	

PAGE NO: (Classification)

119

(Classification)

UNIT OR STAFF SECTION		
TI-TANGO		
ORGANIZATION		
BATTERY "I"-3-12		
OPENED (DTG, Month, year)		CLOSED (DTG, Month, year)
11 1900 MAY		25 1200 MAY

TIME		SER. NO.	DTG	INCIDENTS, MESSAGES, ORDERS, ETC.	ACTION TAKEN M-Maps T-Troops S-Staff F-File
IN	OUT				
			18 2030 H	INTENSIVE FIRE FIGHT NEAR PHU BAI VILLAGE; AZ 1950.	REPORTED TO TI-22
			17 0730 H	RADAR BEACON TEAM MADE CONTACT WITH USS CANBERRA.	
			19 1030 H	HELICOPTER SUPPLY RUN.	
			19 1830 H	ARMY HELICOPTERS ROCKETED + MACHINE GUNNED SUSPECTED ENEMY POSITION BEHIND HILL 153 AZ 4520. OBSERVED 25-30 ARTILLERY ROUNDS (MOSTLY UT) ON SAME POSITION. ORIGIN OF ARTILLERY UNKNOWN. OBSERVED WHAT APPEARED TO BE TROOPS LYING ON THE GROUND ON HILL 153.	KEPT TI-22 INFORMED OF DEVELOPMENTS.
			19 2030 H	OBSERVED FIRE FIGHT AZ 4865 DISTANCE 5000 METERS	REPORTED TO TI-22
			20 1100 H	RECEIVED STONEWALL FROM TI-1	RELAYED TO TI + TI-22
			20 1430 H	HELICOPTER SUPPLY RUN	
			20 1630 H	CAL. MARLATT LEFT HILL TO JOIN RECON PARTY.	
			20 1830 H	BRIEFED BY TI-22 ON OPERATION SCHEDULED FOR 21 MAY.	
			21 0800 H	COMBINED SUNTAN + TINGE INDIA NETS IN SAME LOCATION SO AS TO MONITOR ALL PROCEDURES OF OPERATION.	
			21 2000 H	OBSERVED PHOTO RECONNAISSANCE PLANE TAKING FLASH PICTURES	VERIFIED WITH TI-22

ITEMS	MAX PRICE
CYCLO (cab)	30 P/Hr
BEER	35 P
SOFT DRINK	25 P
WHISKEY (per shot)	60 P
SHORT TIME	200 P
LONG TIME	300 P
SILK SHIRT	250 P
TROUSERS	500 P
STEAK AND FRENCH FRIES	80-100 P
SHRIMP OR FISH	200-250 P
HAIR CUTS	50 P
BIKES, RENT (day)	5 P/Hr
(night)	10 P/Hr

Notes:
1. Settle on price before getting into cyclo.
2. Pay for drinks immediately when served.
3. Do not pay more than the above price.
4. Do not accept less than 130 P per dollar.
5. Do not use American currency.

PRICE LIST WHEN GOING ON LIBERTY INTO HUE CITY

Honors of the 12th Marines

PRESIDENTIAL UNIT CITATION STREAMER

(Vietnam, 12 Jul 1965 - 15 Sep 1967)

NAVY COMMENDATION STREAMER WITH ONE BRONZE STAR

(Empress Augusta Bay and Guam, 1 Nov 1943 - 12 Jan 1944 and 21 Jul 1944 - 10 Aug 1944)
(Iwo Jima, 19 - 28 Feb 1945)

ASIATIC-PACIFIC CAMPAIGN STREAMER WITH FOUR BRONZE STARS

(Treasury-Bougainville Operation, 1 Nov - 15 Dec 1943)
(Consolidation of Solomon Islands, 18 Jan - 3 Jun 1944)
(Marianas Operation, 21 Jul - 15 Aug 1944)
(Iwo Jima Operation, 19 Feb - 15 Mar 1945)

WORLD WAR II VICTORY STREAMER

(1 Sep 1942 - 8 Jan 1946)

NATIONAL DEFENSE SERVICE STREAMER WITH ONE BRONZE STAR

(17 Mar 1952 - 27 Jul 1954)
(1 Jan 1961 - to date)

KOREAN SERVICE STREAMER

(27 Aug 1953 - 27 Jul 1954)

VIETNAM SERVICE STREAMER WITH TWO SLIVER AND ONE BRONZE STARS

(Vietnam Defense Campaign, 10 Apr - 24 Dec 1965)
(Vietnamese Counteroffensive Campaign, 25 Dec 1965 - 30 Jun 1966)
(Vietnamese Counteroffensive Phase II, 1 Jul 1966 - 31 May 1967)
(Vietnamese Counteroffensive Phase III, 1 Jun 1967 - 29 Jan 1968)
(Tet Counteroffensive, 30 Jan - 1 Apr 1968)
(Vietnamese Counteroffensive Phase IV, 2 Apr 1968 - 30 Jun 1968)
(Vietnamese Counteroffensive Phase V, 1 Jul 1968 - 1 Nov 1968)
(Vietnamese Counteroffensive Phase VI, 2 Nov 1968 - 22 Feb 1969)
(Tet 69/Counteroffensive, 23 Feb 1969 - 8 Jun 1969)
(Vietnam, Summer-Fall 1969, 9 Jun 1969 - 31 Oct 1969)
(Vietnam, Winter-Spring 1970, 1 Nov 1969 - 5 Nov 1969)

VIETNAM CROSS OF GALLANTRY WITH PALM

(10 Apr 1965 - 5 Nov 1969)

MERITORIOUS UNIT ~~CITATION~~ COMMENDATION 13-31 JAN '68 IN SUPPORT OF 3/4
NAVY UNIT COMMENDATION 30 APR - 16 MAY '68 3RD MAR DIV

U.S. GOVERNMENT PRINTING OFFICE 1972-714-429/7038

Vietnam(144)

In the early 1960s the international Cold War showed signs
of easing. The Nuclear Test Ban Treaty of 1963 and the
amicability that followed in the wake of the Cuban missile
crisis seemed to foreshadow a possible detente between the
Soviet Union and the United States. But this hopeful progress-
ion was soon dispelled by a series of conflicts in Asia, Africa,
and Latin America, of which the war in Vietnam was the most
dramatic and dangerous. From 1965 to 1972, 447,000 Marines
were to battle in this small country on the rim of the Asian
Continent.

In late February 1965, the decision was made to land a
Marine Expeditionary Brigade (MEB) in Vietnam, whose specific
mission would be to secure the Da Nang Airfield against enemy
intrusion. This mission devolved upon the 9th Marine
Expeditionary Brigade, formed from units of the 3d Marine Division
and the 1st Marine Aircraft Wing. On 8 March, the first
battalion landing team of the brigade, BLT 3/9, came ashore at
Red Beach 2, just north of Da Nang. Included within its support
elements was Battery F, 2d Battalion, 12th Marines. Two days
later, Battery F was joined by Battery A, 1st Battalion, 12th
Marines, which was airlifted to Da Nang from Okinawa to reinforce the 1st Battalion, 3d Marines. Following their arrival,
the batteries were organized into a small artillery group
(Brigade Artillery Group) which provided the artillery support
of the brigade.

The scheme by which the remainder of the 12th Marines was
committed to Vietnam may on the surface look confusing. Prior
to the deployment of additional battalion landing teams to
Vietnam, the regiment assigned its batteries to support their
respective infantry battalions. To ensure that all Marine
installations had the complete spectrum of artillery support,
the 4th Battalion and attached 8-inch Howitzer Battery were
apportioned to selected BLTs. This type of assignment is in
contrast to the direct deployment of complete artillery
battalions, as was done during World War II and Korea. A
discussion of the three combat areas will serve to illustrate
this type of assignment and the initial organizational structures
established.

At Da Nang, elements of the 1st Battalion, 12th Marines
landed in early April and were incorporated into the Brigade
Artillery Group established the previous month. The group
with the inclusion of the 1st Battalion contained three 105mm
howitzer batteries (A/1/12, B/1/12, and F/2/12), a mortar
battery (1/12), a 155mm howitzer battery (L/4/12), an 8-inch
howitzer platoon, and a headquarters battery (Hq Btry, 1/12).
Even though separate in terms of administrative responsibilites,
the group was under the operational control of the 3d Marines.

41

On 6 May, the 9th Marine Expeditionary Brigade was deactivated. The same day III Marine Expeditionary Force(145) was established at Da Nang as the controlling headquarters of Marine troops in the five northernmost provinces of Vietnam which comprised I Corps Tactical Zone. With the arrival of the 2d Battalion, 12th Marines in June and July, each battalion remained separate and under operational control of the 3d and 9th Marines, respectively. On 8 July, the 12th Marine regimental headquarters element joined the 1st and 2d Battalions at Da Nang and assumed its supporting role of the 3d Marine Division, while regaining administrative control of its organic battalions.

With the extension of the Marine area of responsibility to the north, a second enclave was established not far from Hue, the old imperial capital of Vietnam. On 11 April, the 2d Battalion, 3d Marines was landed at Da Nang and the following morning a reinforced company was airlifted to Phu Bai, an airfield and an important Army communications center, seven miles southeast of Hue. Two days later, Marines of the 3d Battalion, 4th Marines (BLT 3/4) moved into the Hue/Phu Bai area in strength. To provide artillery support, Battery I, 3/12 was landed at Da Nang and subsequently shifted to Hue/Phu Bai. On 18 July, Battery I was joined by elements of the 4th Battalion, 12th Marines composed of the organic headquarters battery and one 155mm howitzer battery (M/4/12). To provide additional support, the 107mm mortar battery of the 2d Battalion was attached to the 4th Battalion. Following its arrival, the 4th Battalion was placed in direct support of BLT 3/4 and under the operational control of the 3d Marines, while the administrative control remained with the regimental headquarters which by this time was located at Da Nang.

As the 3d Marine Division was deploying to Vietnam, the 3d Battalion, 12th Marines, 1st Marine Brigade was alerted for immediate transfer to the Far East. On 11 March, 3/12 sailed with the 4th Marines from Ford Island, Hawaii for Okinawa. There, the battalion joined its parent regiment on 27 March after an absence of 10 years.

In late April, the decision was made to secure ground 50 miles south of Da Nang at Chu Lai, in order to construct an expeditionary airfield which would relieve part of the congestion at the Da Nang Airfield. Early the following month, the 3d Marine Amphibious Brigade (composed of the following infantry battalions--1/4, 2/4, and 3/3) came ashore. In support of the brigade, the 3d Battalion, 12th Marines at this time was composed of the following: headquarters battery, 3/12; G and H Batteries, 2/12; 107mm Mortar Battery (Howtar), 3/12; C Battery, 1/12; K Battery, 4/12; and the 1st Platoon, 1st 8-inch Howitzer Battery (SP). In August, with the addition of the 3d Battalion, 11th Marines, both battalions--some 62 pieces in all--joined to form an artillery group under the command of Lieutenant Colonel

42

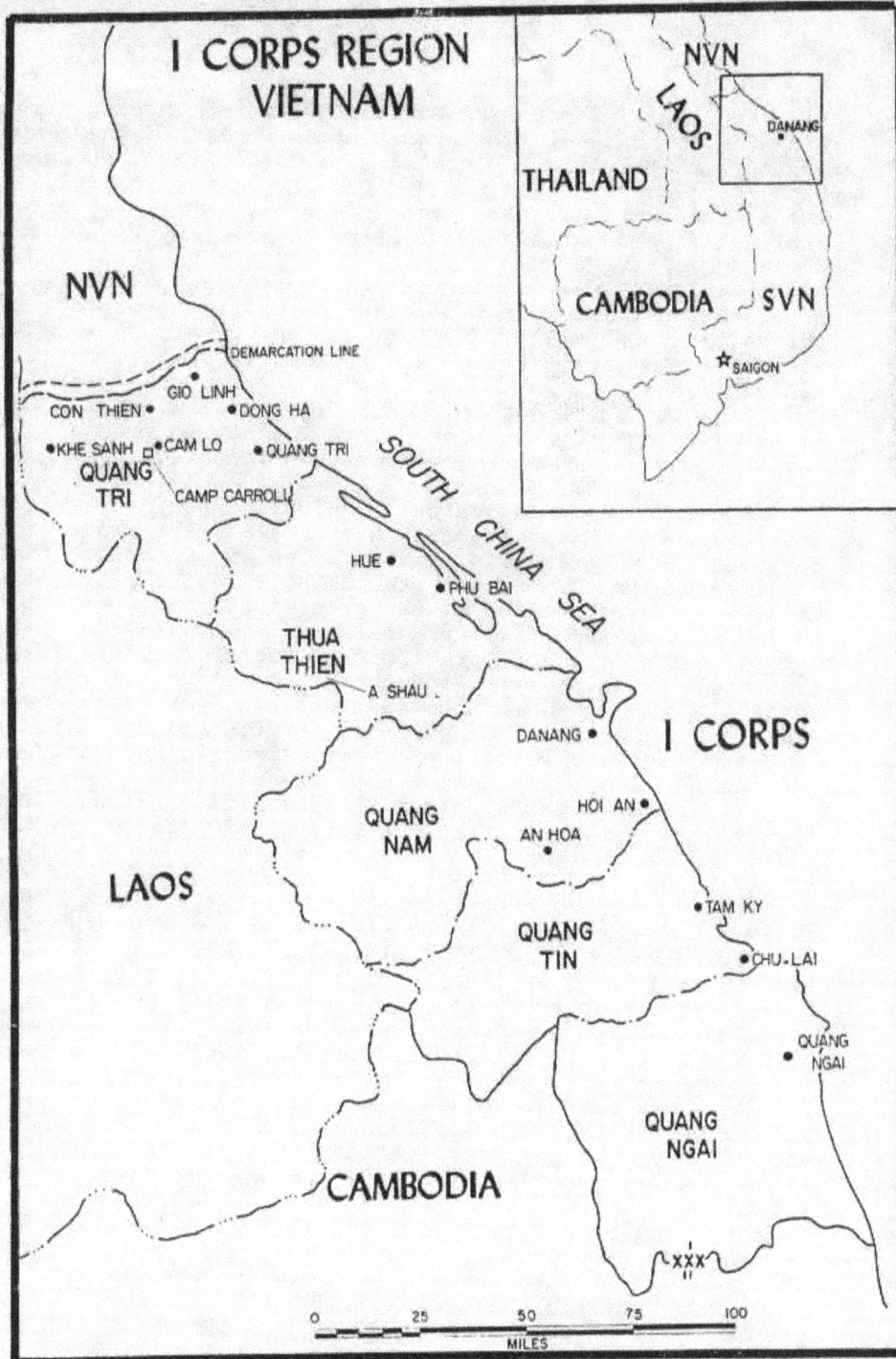

I CORPS REGION
VIETNAM

NVN

DEMARCATION LINE

GIO LINH
CON THIEN • • DONG HA
KHE SANH □ • CAM LO • QUANG TRI
QUANG
TRI
CAMP CARROLL

SOUTH CHINA SEA

HUE •
• PHU BAI

THUA
THIEN
A SHAU

DANANG •

I CORPS

HOI AN •
QUANG
NAM
AN HOA •

LAOS

QUANG
TIN

TAM KY •
CHU-LAI •

QUANG
NGAI •

QUANG
NGAI

CAMBODIA

XXX
II

0   25   50   75   100
MILES

NVN
LAOS
DANANG
THAILAND
CAMBODIA   SVN
☆ SAIGON

43

Leslie L. Page, Commanding Officer, 3/12, which supported the 4th and 7th Marines. The operational control of the group rested with Brigadier General Frederick J. Karch, who was base coordinator at Chu Lai and an artilleryman himself, while the administrative control was lodged with the 12th Marines regimental headquarters at Da Nang.

By early August, the entire regiment with attached units representing the complete spectrum of artillery support within the Marine Corps--light, medium, and heavy weapons--was in Vietnam. The employment of the regiment and its elements was basically the same as its utilization during World War II; direct support of a specific unit or general support of a number of units within the division. This was not to change throughout the course of Marine participation in the Vietnam conflict.

In pursuance of the Marines' defensive posture during the initial period, March to early August 1965, the scope of the regiment's activities was limited. The major thrust of concern was with the improvement of its combat readiness. To achieve this end, the activities of the subordinate battalions at the three enclaves were similarly tailored: preparation of battery and defensive positions placing the largest requirement on time and materials, establishment of communications, vehicle and weapons maintenance, extensive target survey and fire support planning, registration of weapons, service practice, local security, forward observer and enemy aircraft recognition classes, and command post exercises. Since the mission was one of defense, the regiment's combat fire support was limited to the support of patrol and defensive actions aimed at safeguarding the important military installations.

With the approach of the monsoon season, it became "obvious that neither the air war, nor the ground war, not the political war was going well."(146) The initial mission of the 16,000 Marines in I Corps Tactical Area was to secure major bases, in hopes that the South Vietnamese could successsfully carry the brunt of combat operations. These hopes, by late July, had vanished with the concentration of large numbers of Communist forces throughout South Vietnam. In order to stem the immediate threat, General William Westmoreland, Commander, U.S. Military Assistance Command, Vietnam, on 6 August, authorized III MAF to undertake offensive operations in I Corps as well as maintaining the responsibility for base defense.(147)

The first offensive operations in I Corps were small in scale and centered around Chu Lai. In these operations, which turned out to be little more than field exercises against very light resistance, the 4th Marines in conjunction with units of the 2d ARVN Division swept areas west of the airfield. Supporting the infantry operations with landing zone preparations and other

44

forms of direct support, batteries of the 3d Battalion, 12th Marines gained experience that would be invaluable in future operations. Though moderately successful, the operations reemphasized the necessity of coordinating all fire support through a single agency--the Fire Support Coordination Center. In addition, U.S. and ARVN (Army of the Republic of Vietnam) infantry units found that separate and distinct zones of action were necessary, and that advisors with Vietnamese units had to act not only as advisors but as liasion officers between the Vietnamese and American Units.

In mid-August, Marine artillery received its first test in the full-scale offensive operation, STARLITE. For some time there had been intelligence reports which placed the 1st Viet Cong Regiment in prepared positions on the Van Tuong Peninsula, south of Chu Lai. With this information in hand, the 7th Marines jumped into action on 18 August, in what was the first Marine regimental-sized combat operation since the Korean War. In support were approximately 18 pieces of the 3d Battalion, 12th Marines Artillery Group. As Marines of RLT-7 made an amphibious landing and helicopter-borne assaults, a 107mm mortar battery (3/11) of the group was helilifted into the area to provide direct support for infantry elements. General support was provided by K/4/12, which moved into a position within the Tactical Area of Operations, but beyond the Forward Edge of the Battle Area (FEBA) for a period of eight days. This 155mm howitzer battery provided artillery support for Marine and ARVN infantry units during the later stages of the operation.

Throughout the operation the 1st Viet Cong Regiment discovered how devastating Marine artillery could be. During the seven days of the operation, the batteries fired 2,446 rounds of high explosive, white phosphorus, and illumination as missions were called by forward observers with the infantry against enemy fortifications, troop concentrations, suspected assembly areas, and likely avenues of approach. Preparations of landing zones for heliborne assaults, however, provided the batteries with the largest work load during the operation. The most significant single artillery mission occurred when the 107mm Mortar Battery, 3/11 engaged a Viet Cong company marching along a road. The resultant mortar fire left 90 enemy dead.

Operation STARLITE expanded the Marine function beyond that of base defense and marked the beginning of large scale operations as part of a balanced approach in the attempt to eliminate enemy influence. The consolidation of each of the three separate areas of Marine activity through the use of large scale operations, small counterguerrilla operations, and substantial civic action efforts, now allowed Marines to redirect their attention to the traditional Viet Cong strongholds throughout I Corps. In the fall and winter months of 1965, Marines took the war to

45

the enemy with an additional large unit operation, employing rapid maneuver and long range mobility in combination with air, artillery, and naval gunfire resources.

The artillery, although primarily committed to Marine operations, had at the same time other important tasks to support. In attempts to protect villagers and win their confidence, elements of the 12th Marines contributed to the overall village defense effort. An example of one such contribution was made by Battery I, 3/12, at Phu Bai during August 1965. In conferences with chiefs of villages within the range of his howitzers, Captain Donald N. Harmon, Commanding Officer I/3/12, unveiled a plan whereby artillery concentrations could be fired on all possible avenues of enemy access to the villages upon the requests of village chiefs. These concentrations were then individually pre-fired to determine the exact firing data. However, prior to firing-in, the villagers were evacuated to ensure their safety. Once the data was established the village chiefs could then be assured of immediate artillery support to counter enemy attacks. In assessing the effects of the concentrations, Major General Lewis W. Walt, Commanding General of III MAF, commented; "the survey concentration target areas have a definite deterrent effect against the enemy, and have greatly increased the relations which our Marines enjoy with the Vietnamese people in our combined fight against the Viet Cong."(148)

With the consolidation and expansion of Marine areas it soon became apparent that future confrontations between Marine and Viet Cong Main Force units were inevitable. The expansion of the Marine tactical areas at Da Nang, Chu Lai, and Hue/Phu Bai had progressed to such an extent that Marines now constituted an imminent threat to the Viet Cong position and organization. As a result, the enemy had to take action. For two months following STARLITE and Operation PIRANHA, the enemy remained inactive, successfully eluding Marine units. In December 1965, however, a coordinated Marine/ARVN search and destroy operation-- Operation HARVEST MOON--was initiated in the Hiep Duc/Que Son Valley south of Da Nang, to counter the threat posed by the 1st Viet Cong Regiment.

In what was the largest Marine operation since their arrival in March, elements of the 3d and 7th Marines landed in the area by helicopter on 9 December as ARVN elements moved into the area overland. To provide artillery support, a provisional artillery battalion was formed consisting of two 105mm batteries (A/1/11 and F/2/12) and one 155mm battery (M/4/11). An additional 155mm battery, L/4/12, was brought into the operation on the 11th to provide general support for the attacking units, thus reinforcing M/4/11. Three of the batteries deployed beyond the III MAF Tactical Area of Responsibility (TAOR) by motor transport, while the fourth, F/2/12, was helilifted into position; "this was

46

the first time this [had] been accomplished by a Marine 105 Howitzer Battery under combat conditions."(149)

Enemy resistance was heavy, and on 10 December, and again on the 11th, elements of the Special Landing Force of the Seventh Fleet were landed by helicopter in an effort to encircle enemy units. The enemy, in attempting to escape encirclement, began to carry out an effective campaign of harassment. On 19 December, the 2d Battalion, 7th Marines was ambushed by a Viet Cong battalion, as it marched out of the area of operations. In a violent response, Marine air and artillery (M/4/11) dealt a stunning blow to the enemy force. As a result of the 10 day operation, the enemy lost a total of 407 men and a substantial amount of equipment. With the dispersal of the 1st Viet Cong Regiment the forward logistical support areas (LSA) and artillery positions of III MAF were established outside the TAORs and resupplied by motor transport convoys for the first time.

As Marine influence was extended beyond the three enclaves and into hotly contested areas in such operations as DOUBLE EAGLE, MALLARD, GEORGIA, OREGON, ORANGE, JAY, and CHEROKEE, carried out during the first six months of 1966, the basic tactics of artillery support changed little. Throughout the period, the mission of the 12th Marines remained as it had been before; displacement in direct/general support of multi-battalion and small unit operations, and support for base, convoy, and village defense.(150) In more general terms, the 12th provided an artillery umbrella for Marine activities in its assigned area of operation. However, this period was also one in which innovations were added, problems encountered, and refinements in several established techniques were accomplished in response to changing tactical situations and developments.

As in previous wars where artillery had been put to extensive use in populated areas, the rules of engagement had to be tailored to meet the situation. The main effort in Vietnam was aimed at the defeat of Communist main force units and the elimination of the Viet Cong infrastructure throughout the country. Concurrent with this effort was the desire to win the confidence of the people. Thus, in determining where and how artillery was to be used, both the military and the psychological effect upon the population had to be considered. Had artillery been used indiscriminately and only with the thought of achieving momentary military advantage at the expense of noncombatants, the long-term pacification effort would have been lost. As a result, when artillery was used in preparations for landing zones, reconnaissance by fire, and harassing and interdiction fires, it had to be used discriminately so as to minimize the destruction of property and civilian casualties. If it were not, such unrestrained use of artillery would be the subject of Communist exploitation. When an operation was slated for a certain area,

47

liaison was established early with South Vietnamese military and civilian officials, often times down to the village level, to assist in problems that might arise during the operation. This type of cooperation greatly facilitated the planning of artillery fires and the lessening of noncombatant casualties. Both the coordination and restraints exercised by the artillery in Vietnam should not be construed as a limit upon its response to hostile actions. Intense and precise planning would eliminate the over use of artillery. In the last analysis, however, the field commander and the fire support coordination center would be the final judges when to call upon supporting arms fire.

An additional facet in the control of supporting arms was the development of SAV-A-PLANE. Due to the problem of crowded air space in certain areas of Vietnam, particularly along Route 1 in I Corps, an artillery unit operating within the area had to contend with innumerable aircraft--from helicopters to commercial airliners--which penetrated its zone of action. To lessen the competition for air space and prevent the accidental shooting down of a friendly aircraft, the SAV-A-PLANE technique was developed. The technique involved a message that was sent indicating the location of the target, the location of the artillery (or naval gunfire) unit, the time the fire was to commence, and the maximum ordinate of the trajectory. After this information was supplied it was the responsibility of the pilot to avoid the firing area. To further ensure that friendly aircraft were not shot out of the air by Allied artillery and naval gunfire, the traditional use of an aircraft sentry at a battery position was employed. In addition, the forward artillery observer was co-located with the forward air controller to coordinate artillery fire with airstrikes and made it possible for the immediate lifting or shifting of artillery fires should a friendly aircraft stray into the zone of fire.

In Vietnam, the employment of a battery as a separate and distinct unit in providing direct support for infantry units was developed to the fullest. From the first introduction of Marine combat forces in March 1965, the battery became the basic unit of support. Its versatility in terms of separate fire direction and communications capability, rapid deployment by helicopter, and 360 degree fire capacity, enabled a single battery to provide support to the infantry normally supported by a battalion in a conventional war.

Due to the flexibility of the artillery battery, much innovation and experimentation as to the tactical use of artillery was permitted. In an effort to improve artillery support, tried practices were strengthened and expanded, and new ones developed to meet changing situations. Consequently, much energy was expended to seek new methods of increasing the rapid delivery and accuracy of artillery fires. Prior to the deployment of

48

an infantry unit, artillery fires would be percisely planned to cover the insertion, protection, orientation, and for the extraction of the unit should it become necessary. Once a forward observer communicated his request for artillery support, usually all that was needed was the clearance to fire.

As Marine units extended their areas of responsibility into what had hitherto been Viet Cong sanctuaries or strongholds, reconnaissance teams were sent beyond the TAORs. The primary mission of these teams (code named STING-RAY) was to gather intelligence about enemy troop movements, strong points, and assembly areas. However, it soon became apparent that the team could effectively direct air and artillery strikes on lucrative enemy targets without compromising their positions. The platoon or team leader now became the extension of the forward observer usually based with an infantry unit of a larger size. In addition, the effects of the STING-RAY operations negated the thought that the Vietnamese hinterlands would always be a Viet Cong reserve. A corollary development of the STING-RAY technique was that of artillery ambushes. Once a team had been inserted, it would pick out trails and stream fording points of likely Viet Cong traffic. Artillery would then be targeted on the routes. If enemy groups were observed, the artillery response was rapid and deadly.(151)

A type of combat reminiscent of the Japanese counterattacks on Guam, was experienced by artillerymen of the 12th Marines throughout the course of their participation in the Vietnam conflict. As the tactical areas of Marine responsibility extended and artillery was deployed into less secure areas to support operations, the relative security of the larger military installations was left behind. Once in battery positions away from the major bases, the batteries were subjected to an increased number of short and violent Viet Cong attacks carried out under the cover of darkness. The first major attack occurred on the night of 18 April 1966, as the positions of K/4/12 and A/1/11, northwest of Da Nang, were hit by a mortar and ground attack.(152) At 0145, Battery K received enemy mortar and small arms rounds and responded with small arms fire and direct fire from its 155mm howitzers (SP). At approximately the same time A/1/11 came under heavy attack by an estimated Viet Cong company (50-60 men). Armed with bangalore torpedoes, small arms, satchel charges, and grenades, the lightly clad enemy force immediately penetrated the perimeter and overran the security outposts. Once inside the battery perimeter, the force destroyed two howitzers, and damaged the remaining pieces. At 0204 illumination was requested from A/1/12 and Mortar Battery, 1/12 by radio since all wire communications were cut prior to the attack. Due to the surprise and swiftness by which the attack was carried out, only one fire mission against the attacking force was completed. The attack subsided at approximately 0500; in its wake the enemy force left 15 killed, while the

49

defenders suffered 5 killed and 28 wounded. The following morning elements of the 1st Battalion, 3d Marines swept the area, but with negative results.(153) This type of attack was to persist as Marines continued to leave secure areas in search of an elusive enemy. At times these attacks resulted in heavy casualties on both sides.

The influx of large contingents of American forces into South Vietnam during 1965 and their early successes reversed the military situation. By mid-1966, the precarious political situation was partially stabilized, thus reducing the chances of a quick Communist victory. Although the North Vietnamese made no changes in basic aims, they did open a new front just south of the Demilitarized Zone (DMZ) by invading the area in division strength and increasing infiltration throughout other areas of South Vietnam. Many Allied commanders believed that by extending the war into the DMZ area the North Vietnamese hoped to neutralize the expansion of Marine influence in I Corps, to take the pressure off Viet Cong units operating farther south by diverting U.S. attention to the northern sector of Vietnam, and to disrupt the pacification program.

As increasing amounts of intelligence information were received, III MAF conducted several battalion-sized operations in Quang Tri Province during May and early June, but without success. In early July, solid intelligence was received which placed several large North Vietnamese regular units just south of the DMZ. As General Lewis Walt later noted:

> This was a turning point in the conflict. Until
> early 1966 my men had been widely dispersed,
> exercising the greatest amount of security over
> the greatest number of people, concentrating only
> when we found Viet Cong Main Force units trying
> to bolster the hapless and struggling guerrilla,
> or to protect our most vital installations against
> guerrilla attack. Now we were in a situation
> similar to that in Korea in 1950--an army coming
> down from the north to seize and hold ground.(154)

Once the enemy's intentions became known to U.S. military commanders, it was decided in early July to shift the necessary Marine forces from southern I Corps into Quang Tri Province to stem North Vietnamese infiltration, and halt the enemy's advance.

Before possible North Vietnamese offensive operations could be launched, five Marine infantry battalions (2/1, 2/4, 3/4, 1/3, and 1/1), designated Task Force Delta, and an equal number of ARVN units converged on areas in Quang Tri Province. To provide artillery support the 3d Battalion, 12th Marines (-)(Rein) moved from Phu Bai to the Dong Ha area on 12-13 July to join H/3/12 which had displaced to the area the previous month. On

50

15 July, Operation HASTINGS, the largest coordinated offensive operation up to that time, was initiated. Under the protective cover of 3/12, infantry elements of the combined force were inserted into landing zones, established blocking positions along enemy trails, and initiated search and destroy operations throughout the assigned area. The following day, the Seventh Fleet Special Landing Force began Operation DECKHOUSE II which was slated to protect the seaward flanks of the main operation. As Task Force Delta was bolstered by SLF units, additional batteries (11th Marines) were brought in to reinforce the fires of 3/12.

Once underway, HASTINGS was characterized by a number of sharp, violent, small unit engagements with an occasional large encounter. In all instances, 3/12 in combination with other supporting arms accounted for the majority of the 824 enemy casualties. On 3 August, Operation HASTINGS terminated as the remnants of North Vietnamese regular units retreated back across the DMZ or into sanctuaries in Laos.

With the termination of HASTINGS, a new operation, PRAIRIE, was begun in the same area. Slated to seek out and destroy the remaining North Vietnamese Army (NVA) troops and prevent further infiltration attempts, additional infantry battalions and artillery batteries were added to this search and destroy operation under the control of the 4th Marines. Throughout August and September, 3/12 which had operational control over approximately nine batteries, supported the various activities of the infantry battalions. Fire missions during this period were concerned with the reduction of enemy fortifications, troops, and infiltration routes, and the support of reconnaissance teams operating in the southern and western reaches of Quang Tri Province. In several instances, fire missions undertaken as a result of a reconnaissance team's request were instrumental in inflicting heavy enemy casualties.

In early October, as Operation PRAIRIE was expanded, several major changes in the location and organization of the regiment took place. As the responsibility for the Da Nang TAOR was passed to the 1st Marine Division and the 3d Marine Division shifted its forces to the north, the 12th Marine regimental headquarters with its 1st and 4th Battalions moved by truck and landing craft to the Dong Ha area. With the departure of the 12th Marines (-)(Rein), the 2d Battalion, 12th Marines was assigned on 10 October to the 1st Division as its component batteries continued to participate in combat operations south and west of Da Nang. Upon the arrival of the regiment at Dong Ha, it was positioned into a triangular operational area near the DMZ cornered by Dong Ha, Camp J.J. Carroll, and Cam Lo, with several intermediate positions. Following redeployment, the regiment assumed control of two Army battalions--1st Battalion, 40th Artillery (105mm howitzers (SP)) and 2d Battalion, 94th

51

Cannoneers of 12th Marines supporting Operation PRAIRIE, October 1966. (USMC Photo #A187927)

A 155mm howitzer (self-propelled) of Battery M, 4/12 fires on enemy positions near Phu Bai, Republic of Vietnam. (USMC Photo #A188024)

Artillery (175mm guns (SP))--which were to act as a general support element of the division. With the increased capability for long-range support provided by the 175mm guns, the 12th now created an artillery umbrella stretching from the South Vietnam/Laos border to the South China Sea.

As units of the 12th Marines moved into northern I Corps, the artillery support for the Phu Bai TAOR was temporarily diminished. With the movement of 3/12 in July 1966, 4th Marine units operating within the TAOR were provided support by two to three batteries under the direction of 3/12 Rear. In October, a provisional artillery battalion was formed at Phu Bai incorporating the three batteries from the 1st, 2d, and 3d Battalions, and an additional battery of 155mm self-propelled howitzers. The Provisional Artillery unit supported combat operations within the Phu Bai TAOR until 17 December when 4/12 headquarters element displaced to Phu Bai and in the process absorbed the provisional battalion.

The end of 1966 found the 12th Marines centered in three locations and supporting three major Marine operations. South of Da Nang, elements of the 2d Battalion under the operational control of the 11th Marines, 1st Marine Division continued to support operations in the An Hoa area. In northern I Corps, the remaining elements of the 12th Marines were divided into two camps; one at Phu Bai and the other at Dong Ha. In the Phu Bai TAOR elements of the 3d Battalion which had displaced temporarily to the area, and the 4th Battalion, supported Operation CHINOOK which was initiated in mid-December to block enemy infiltration routes into the coastal plains and the city of Hue. This operation was to continue into early February. Further north, batteries of the 1st, 3d (-), and 4th Battalions, reinforced by 1/40 and 2/94 continued to support Operation PRAIRIE. In conjunction with combat operations in Vietnam, several batteries of the regiment were withdrawn, sent to Okinawa to reequip and retrain, and then joined the battalion landing teams of the Seventh Fleet. This practice had been abandoned in June of 1965, but was reinstituted as elements of the 5th Marine Division were brought into Vietnam one year later.

General William Westmoreland summed up the situation in Vietnam of early 1967 by indicating that "the momentum gained by the end of 1966 was carried over into 1967. Additional troops and other valuable resources enable the scope and pace of our offensive operations to increase steadily throughout the year."(155) In specific reference to I Corps Tactical Zone, General Westmoreland continued:

> In the northern part of the I Corps, our objectives
> for 1967 were to meet and defeat North Vietnam's
> invasion through the DMZ and Laos, to interdict the
> enemy's infiltration routes in South Vietnam, and to

neutralize his base areas near the coastal plain,
which provided his guerrilla forces much of their
support. Equally important in the southern portion
of the corps zone was the protection of our base
areas and the lines of communication that enabled
the government to extend its control.(156)

For the 12th Marines, which at this time was in support of both
the 1st and 3d Marine Divisions, the course for 1967 was set.

Throughout the first three months of 1967 elements of the
1st (-), 3d (-), and 4th (-) Battalions, and attached Army
artillery units, continued to provide support for the PRAIRIE
and CHINOOK series of operations, ARVN/GVN forces, and patrol
activities of the 3d Reconnaissance Battalion. With the con-
clusion of the monsoon season in early February, enemy contact
began to increase as the North Vietnamese stepped up attempts
to infiltrate men and equipment into the south. In addition,
aerial reconnaissance during this period located evidence of
large NVA troop and material concentrations north of the Ben
Hai River which separates North Vietnam from the South and bi-
sects the Demilitarized Zone. As a result, III MAF requested
and received authorization in late February to conduct artillery
fire missions against purely military targets in and north of
the DMZ. This authority was granted in order to supplement
airstrikes against military targets in the DMZ during periods
of reduced visibility, to provide protection for long-range
reconnaissance flights by destroying known antiaircraft sites,
and to disrupt lines of communication over which the North
Vietnamese were resupplying their units in the DMZ and northern
Quang Tri Province. In response to the authorization, the 12th
Marines on 26 February activated the 1st Composite Provisional
Battalion. Composed of a detachment from Headquarters Battery,
1/12, and Batteries C/1/12 and B/2/94, the battalion moved the
same date to the Gio Linh outpost--approximately one mile south
of the DMZ--where it initiated Operation HIGHRISE (artillery
fires targeted within the DMZ and North Vietnam). Another
position was established further west at Cam Lo the following
month.

During March and early April 1967, enemy forces within the
DMZ and other sectors of Quang Tri Province increased the
pressure on Marine units and installations. With the advent of
the dry summer months in I Corps, the North Vietnamese hoped
to increase the infiltration rate, thus drawing Marine forces
away from the lowlands and into the mountains. In response, an
Army task force was deployed to the Chu Lai area. The arrival
of Army troops in Quang Ngai Province allowed the 7th Marines
to move north from Chu Lai to Da Nang, thus freeing the 9th
Marines and permitting their northward deployment. In conjunction, the 2d Battalion, 12th Marines moved northward from Da
Nang and established a command post at Dong Ha on 22 April.

54

The following day the 2d Battalion rejoined the regiment and continued its operational role of directly supporting the 9th Marines.

The realignment of Marine forces in northern I Corps throughout March and April was accomplished at the beginning of a critical period in the Vietnam war. No longer were enemy forces willing to take the incessant beatings the Marines were giving them; a significant and clear-cut victory was needed. On the morning of 24 April, what began as a brief patrol engagement near the small outpost of Khe Sanh soon mushroomed into a series of intense battles that lasted until 12 May. This engagement seemed to have prematurely revealed the enemy's plans of attacking the Khe Sanh base in a fashion similar to that of the Battle of Dien Bien Phu. (157) The following day the outpost was reinforced by the 3d Battalion, 3d Marines which then proceeded to engage entrenched enemy forces in order to secure the commanding ground west of the base. Under the cover of artillery fires provided by B/1/12 and F/2/12 at Khe Sanh and airstrikes of the 1st Marine Aircraft Wing, 3d Marine infantry companies successively secured Hills 861 and 881. By 12 May the enemy's threat to Khe Sanh had been broken and the following day the 26th Marines replaced the 3d Marines. As the first battle of Khe Sanh concluded, B/1/12 was withdrawn and replaced by A/1/13. The two batteries at Khe Sanh were then designated the Provisional Artillery Group: Khe Sanh, and attached to the 26th Marines in order to provide direct support for Operation CROCKETT.

As Operation CROCKETT sought to eliminate the remaining NVA forces in the northwestern sector of Quang Tri Province, Marine, ARVN, and Seventh Fleet SLF forces combined to conduct multiple attacks in the DMZ, south of the Ben Hai River in late May. For several months the NVA had been using the DMZ as an infiltration and staging area for ground, rocket, and artillery attacks on Marine positions to the south. Therefore, directives were issued authorizing friendly forces to enter the DMZ (areas south of the Ben Hai River) and destroy enemy units, installations, and supplies, in addition to establishing a free-fire zone following the evacuation of all area noncombatants. As infantry elements scoured the DMZ area, seven batteries of the 12th Marines combined with air and naval gunfire resources to suppress heavy enemy harassing fires and destroy long suspected enemy mortar and artillery sites which had pounded Marine positions close to the DMZ for some time. With the termination of the operations (HICKORY/LAM SON 54/BEAU CHARGER) on 28 May, the enemy's undisputed hold on the DMZ area south of the Ben Hai River was crushed for the time being.

During Operations HICKORY/BEAU CHARGER, the enemy tried a new tactic in an attempt to destroy Marines forces, but it failed due to the alert artillerymen of the 12th Marines. By

55

monitoring radio transmissions between BLT 1/3 and the 12th
Marines FSCC (Fire Support Coordination Center) at Dong Ha, the
enemy became familiar with local requests for fire support.
In one instance a request was received at the 12th FSCC asking
for a fire mission, but for some reason the originator used
the land-line call sign instead of the radio call signal. The
puzzled FSCC personnel in return demanded confirmation, but
received no reply. A subsequent examination of the target coordinates revealed that the enemy was trying to get Marine
artillery to fire into the middle of 1/3's position. The fire
mission, needless to say, was ignored. A similar situation
had occurred during Operation PRAIRIE the previous year. In
the midst of a fire mission by a 155mm battery of the 4th
Battalion, a request was received demanding a cease-fire and
giving new coordinates for the fire mission. A quick check by
battalion FDC personnel revealed that the target was in the
middle of known Marine positions. A mission was fired, but not
at the coordinates given. Instead, Marine 8-inch howitzers
fired on the suspected radio location, and it was not heard from
again.(158)

The remainder of 1967 saw batteries of the 12th Marines
supporting numerous operations within the two northernmost
provinces of South Vietnam. In Thua Thien Province, cannoneers
of the 12th countered enemy movement in such areas as the A Shau
Valley. To the north in Quang Tri Province, batteries continued
to support Marine operations against heavy enemy pressure at
such places as Khe Sanh, Con Thien, and Cam Lo. It was for
actions during this period that a member of Battery H, 3d
Battalion, 12th Marines was awarded the nation's highest honor--
the Medal of Honor. In the early morning hours of 14 October,
while occupying a defensive position which protected a vital
bridge on the road between Con Thien and Cam Lo, the 2d Battalion,
4th Marines came under a heavy mortar and artillery attack
followed by a concerted ground assault by an estimated NVA
battalion.(159) The enemy penetrated the defensive perimeter and
brought heavy fire upon the battalion command post wounding
among others, Sergeant Paul H. Foster, fire support coordination
chief, H/3/12. Although wounded, Sergeant Foster continued to
direct accurate mortar and artillery fire upon the advancing
enemy force. As the fight continued, a hand grenade landed in
the position occupied by himself and five other Marines. Without
thought of his own safety, Sergeant Foster threw his armored vest
and then himself over the grenade and absorbed the entire blast.
As a result, Sergeant Foster received severe wounds of which he
later died. On 20 June 1969, President Richard M. Nixon
posthumously awarded the Medal of Honor to Sergeant Foster.

The year 1967, in addition to being one in which the enemy
attempted to make northern I Corps the battle ground, was also
one of modernization and expansion for the 12th Marines. In
July, the 12th received a new piece of equipment that was to

56

become standard--the Field Artillery Digital Computer (FADAC).
Prior to its arrival, all computations of firing data had been
accomplished by hand; now with the FADAC the process of providing
a firing battery with accurate data was accelerated. The net
effect of the computer was to lessen reaction time from the
request for fire support to impact of the round on target, while
still maintaining complete accuracy.

Throughout the first five months of 1967, Marine installations in areas south of the DMZ were subjected to heavy enemy
mortar, artillery, and rocket attacks. The largest problem in
countering the enemy artillery activity was in locating the
enemy guns. In order to upgrade the regiment's counterbattery
program, Section C, 2d Target Acquisition Battery (USA) was
attached to the 12th Marines on 27 October. This unit soon
established flash, sound, and radar installations at forward
outposts, thus increasing the regiment's capability to perform
its counterbattery/mortar mission. In November the regiment
was able to report that it now possessed "the capability to
engage artillery/mortar targets with a relatively high assurance
of achieving neutralization of the target."(160) With the
addition of two units which came under the regiment's operational
control during the latter part of 1967, the 12th Marines by
December had become the largest de facto regiment in the history
of the Marine Corps.(161) In addition to its organic battalions--
1st, 2d, 3d, and 4th--the 12th Marines then controlled the 1st
Battalion, 11th Marines; 1st Battalion, 13th Marines; 1st 8-
inch Howitzer Battery; 5th 155mm Gun Battery; 1st Searchlight
Battery; and two provisional 155mm howitzer batteries. The
regiment also controlled several Army units of the 108th Field
Artillery Group which included the 8th Battalion, 4th Artillery;
1st Battalion, 40th Artillery; and the 2d Battalion, 94th
Artillery.

In late 1967 and the first months of 1968, the strategy and
tactics of the North Vietnamese went through a subtle change.
The combination of the enemy's ineffectiveness in the northern
provinces and the growing strength of the South Vietnamese
forced the leaders in Hanoi to abandon their long-range strategy
of defeating Free World forces in the field and adopt the policy
of bringing "their military power to bear directly on their main
objective--the people and the government of South Vietnam--
regardless of cost."(162) In December 1967, information was
received and later verified which indicated massive enemy troop
movement toward the main centers of population--Saigon, Da Nang,
and Hue--and areas south of the Demilitarized Zone, and that
major enemy offensive operations would be undertaken prior to
or immediately following the Vietnamese Lunar New Year--Tet.
Based on the intelligence information and the increasing number
of enemy initiated incidents, U.S. military commanders affected
a realignment of U.S. ground units throughout South Vietnam to
meet the growing enemy threats. As part of the realignment,

57

the 3d and 4th Battalions, 12th Marines deployed from the Hue/
Phu Bai TAOR to Quang Tri Province in mid-January where they
joined the remainder of the regiment.

The repositioning of U.S. ground troops could not have
come at a more auspicious moment. With the arrival of the Vietnamese New Year celebrations on 29 January, the enemy launched
a well coordinated series of major attacks against friendly
military installations, lines of communication, and principle
Vietnamese cities and administrative centers. Even before the
Tet holidays Marines in northern I Corps were actively engaging
enemy forces. On 20 January, a Marine company made contact
with an entrenched North Vietnamese battalion north of Khe Sanh.
Reinforcements were inserted into the area and the second battle
for Khe Sanh began. The following day several hill outposts
and the base itself came under a heavy, unrelenting enemy
mortar, rocket, and artillery barrage. For the next three
months the North Vietnamese lashed out time and time again in
an effort to drive the Marines from the base and ultimately from
the area. In every instance the Marines tightened their defenses
and responded with overwhelming massed artillery fires and coordinated air support. "By 1 April the Tet offensive was over,
the battle for Hue was fought and won, and the siege of Khe
Sanh had just about petered out."(163)

As the 1st Battalion, 13th Marines(164) supported operations
in the Khe Sanh area, the remaining elements of the regiment
continued to support Marine, ARVN, and U.S. Army forces engaged
in combat operations within Quang Tri Province. Simultaneously,
batteries located at combat bases within range of the DMZ (Gio
Linh, and Cam Lo) continued to shell military targets within
the zone and the southern panhandle of North Vietnam. Late in
1967, at the direction of the 3d Marine Division Commanding
General, a study was initiated to develop a system that would
provide for more efficient management, allocation, application,
and coordination of supporting arms employment with respect to
the DMZ. Initially, there had been little coordination in the
utilization of artillery, naval gunfire, and fixed-wing aircraft in destroying enemy fortifications, and positions from
which artillery and rocket attacks were launched against Allied
installations in northern Quang Tri Province. All that was
done was to increase the counterbattery fire program. The
ineffectiveness of this type of response stemmed from three
problems: (1) imprecision in locating enemy guns; (2) lack
of observation in order to adjust fires; and (3) the late,
incomplete, and often times negative results. To facilitate
the management of the vast arsenal of supporting arms available,
the Fire Support Information Center (FSIC)(165) was activated.
The main function of the FSIC was to give an "orderly, graphic
presentation of supporting arms information, enabling the Fire
Support Coordinator to clearly identify problem areas, and
allocated his resources toward their solution."(166) In

simplified terms, the FSIC acted as a clearing house for all
information pertinent to supporting arms, and facilitated the
"deliberate advance planning of offensive operations exclusively
by supporting arms.'"(167)

With the termination of the monsoon season in early April,
decisions were made to begin a three-phase counteroffensive
operation. The primary objectives of the counteroffensive were
the relief of Khe Sanh which was being resupplied at that
time only by air, a raid into the A Shau Valley in Thua Thien
Province, and an attack into the DMZ. On 1 April, a coordinated
Marine, ARVN, U.S. Army operation was launched to reestablish
land contact with the Khe Sanh base. Light resistance was met
as the 1st Marines moved overland in an effort to reopen Route
9. At the same time an ARVN airborne battalion and the 3d
Brigade, 1st Air Cavalry Division moved in a successively
southward direction, leap-frogging from position to position.
On 4 April, the 26th Marines attacked from the Khe Sanh base
itself, linking up with the relief forces two days later. By
9 April, the land route to Khe Sanh was clear. In late April,
the 1st Marines took over responsibility for the base's defense,
and the 1st Battalion, 11th Marines relieved the 1st Battalion,
13th Marines. With the relief of the base accomplished, III
MAF then turned its attention to the other two objectives.

By the end of May, several fresh enemy regiments had moved
into the Khe Sanh area and a major attack was imminent. Instead
of relying on several established positions from which infantry
units covered by artillery support would venture out in search
of the enemy, it was decided to employ a number of highly mobile
infantry-artillery teams. The plan of operation involved the
establishment of several large landing zones and fire support
bases (FSB) that would provide the infantry maneuver elements
with close, continuous artillery coverage. On 3 June, 1/4 moved
into the area after five days of air and artillery preparations
and established a landing zone into which A/1/12 was moved two
days later. Throughout the succeeding 13 days additional
landing zones and fire bases were carved out of the double
canopy jungle. Since the landing zones and bases were not
within the proximity of land routes, the infantry and artillery
elements were totally dependent upon the helicopter for resupply.
The importance of this action as part of the overall III MAF
Operation SCOTLAND II, was that "it was the first use of
mountain-top bases by the 3d Marine Division and they worked
well."(168)

The concept of establishing artillery fire support bases
was not revolutionary. In late 1965 during Operation HARVEST
MOON, artillery batteries were transported by helicopter to
forward positions in order to effectively cover the infantry's
area of operation. Initially, however, these forward artillery
positions were tied to locations near roads which facilitated

A Marine CH-53 (Sea Stallion) delivering an externally loaded 105mm howitzer to FSB Fuller, location of Battery H, 3/12. (Photo courtesy of Mr. Tom Bartlett, Leatherneck)

60

their construction and resupply. In early 1968, with improved logistics, additional troops, and the greater availability of helicopter resources in northern I Corps, the 3d Marine Division now employed heliborne infantry supported by quickly established, mutually supporting fire bases. With these bases, the division was then able to move its maneuver elements in a leap-frog manner over the great expanse of mountainous terrain without a loss of artillery support.

The fire support base itself is "essentially a forward artillery position located atop a key terrain feature which can be defended by a minimum of infantry personnel."(169) The construction of an artillery fire base begins with the careful selection of a landing zone (LZ). Once the LZ is selected intensive artillery and airstrikes are directed at the proposed site to discourage enemy troops and clear the area of obstacles. Following the preparations a reconnaissance team or a security force accompanied by an engineer unit is inserted to carry out the initial clearing of the LZ. After the base is cleared and the primary construction completed, the artillery pieces are brought in by helicopter and the fire support base is activated. (170)

In addition to exercising tactical fire direction and providing fire support for Marine, U.S. Army, and ARVN forces engaged in combat operations within Quang Tri Province during the remainder of 1968, elements of the 12th Marines (-)(171) continued to conduct a number of artillery raids in the DMZ and the southern panhandle of North Vietnam. The major raid of 1968 began 1 July as units of the regiment combined with Marine, Navy, and Air Force attack aircraft; B-52s of the Strategic Air Command; and ships of the Seventh Fleet, to destroy enemy sanctuaries and artillery positions in the DMZ area. The seven-day barrage created by Operation THOR was quickly exploited by infantry elements which invested areas south of the DMZ, destroying enemy forces, fortifications, and supply caches. In addition, the operation was successful in regaining control of the DMZ to the extent that incoming enemy fire was sharply reduced and Allied aerial observers were once again free to fly over the zone.

What began as a year of intense combat activity in I Corps ended with the enemy pulling back his main force units into sanctuaries in Laos and North Vietnam. For the 12th Marines the period was marked by a contrast in the number of positions occupied by firing batteries. At the beginning of the year, the 12th Marines supported a large area of operation and had under its operational control 35 firing units situated at 12 locations from Gio Linh to Phu Bai. But a series of developments during the year reduced the number of firing units while increasing the number of positions. The first occurred in April when the regiment lost operational control of several Army units as the

61

108th Field Artillery Group was transferred to the control of the Provisional Corps, Vietnam (later XXIV Corps) at Phu Bai. The second took place in July following the reduction of the area of operation to the approximate boundaries of Quang Tri Province, when the accelerated program of fire support base construction was begun. As a result of these two developments, the 12th Marines by December controlled 22 firing units situated at 21 locations throughout Quang Tri Province. This dispersal and reduction in the number of units had little effect upon the performance of the regiment's mission, even though at times this imposed an increased burden on the remaining units. To increase the firepower available to the regiment on fire support bases and to compensate for the loss of long-range support, additional towed 155mm howitzers were added during August to augment the regiment's existing 155mm howitzers. By the end of 1968, with the increased mobility of the regiment and the ceasefire in and north of the DMZ, artillery support requirements remained relatively steady, despite the reduction in the number of firing batteries assigned to the 12th Marines.

The momentum achieved by the success of 3d Marine Division operations in northern I Corps during 1968 was expanded during 1969. Combat operations, though fewer in number, carried the fight to the enemy's western base areas, cutting his lines of communication and supply, destroying his hidden war material, and resulting in a greater number of enemy casualties. The beginning of the regiment's fifth and final year in Vietnam saw the 12th Marines again providing tactical fire direction and coordinated fire support for Marine, U.S. Army, and ARVN forces engaged in combat operations within and near Quang Tri Province. These forces included the 3d Marine Division (-) (Rein), 101st Airbourne Division (April-June), river patrol craft of Task Force Clearwater, force reconnaissance teams, combined action platoons, 1st Brigade, 5th Mechanized Infantry Division, and elements of the 1st and 2d ARVN Regiments operating within the 3d Marine Division's area of operation.

The first major operation of 1969 began on 22 January as units of the 9th Marines, 2d ARVN Regiment, and 2d Battalion, 12th Marines combined to initiate Operation DEWEY CANYON in the western reaches of Quang Tri and Thua Thien Provinces. The operation was divided into three distinct phases: (1) the displacement of maneuver elements to the area of operation and the construction of mutually supporting fire bases; (2) local saturation patrols; and (3) a conventional search and clear operation in the area. The first phase of the operation began as 9th Marines units were inserted into the area of operation, reopening several previously abandoned fire bases, and began construction on FSB Cunningham. As the operation progressed, FSB Cunningham became its center, not only in terms of containing the control command posts, but in terms of its critical location. The fire support base was situated in the center of the area of

62

A Marine UH-1E helicopter touches down at FSB Cunningham, as
artillerymen of the 12th Marines support 9th Marine units
during Operation DEWEY CANYON. (USMC Photo #A192655)

A 105mm howitzer of Battery E, 2/12 at Con Thien firing in
support of the 1st Battalion, 1st Marines. (USMC Photo #371011)

63

operation and its 11 kilometer artillery fan extended south and
southwest to the limits of Area of Operation (AO)(172). Because
of its strategic location, Cunningham contained as many as
five artillery batteries--two 105mm, two 155mm, and one 4.2-
inch mortar battery--at one time.

Several problems were encountered by the 2d Battalion as
Phase II and III progressed. The first was the problem of resupply. By early February, the northeastern monsoon was at its
height. Weather for helicopter operations was marginal at best.
The problem of resupplying forward support bases became acute.
By February the 2d Battalion had only enough rations to supply
one meal per day per man, and ammunition was scarce. Eventually
resupply was accomplished by helicopter and fixed-wing air drops.
The second problem was that of the large number of assaults by
fire and by ground attacks against artillery fire bases. Since
the operation was being conducted within close proximity of the
Laotian border, the enemy was able to shell Allied fire bases
from positions within Laos which were outside the range of
Allied artillery. Similarly, enemy forces were able to launch
a series of ground attacks against the majority of active bases
and then retreat southwest into Laos.

The success of Operation DEWEY CANYON--which terminated on
18 March--can be measured not only by the quantity of enemy
casualties and equipment destroyed or captured, but also by
the cooperation and coordination achieved between Marine and
ARVN elements and the relationships of intra-service units.
In July 1968, Major General Raymond G. Davis, Commanding General,
3d Marine Division, realigned the batteries, companies, battalions,
and regiments of the division to restore unit cohesiveness and
integrity. Previously, battalions and regiments rarely were
composed of their organic subordinate or support units.(173)
Operation DEWEY CANYON witnessed the completion of this realignment process.

Following the termination of Operation DEWEY CANYON, the
regiment continued to support combat operations, and conduct
unobserved artillery missions against military targets in the
southern portion of the DMZ and throughout Quang Tri Province.
The unattended ground sensor capability which was added to the
division during the previous year proved to be extremely valuable during 1969 in detecting enemy presence and movement
throughout the area of operation. No longer was the regiment
wholly dependent upon target acquisition information obtained
from ground and aerial observation. With the addition of this
family of sophisticated electronic devices, the regiment
improved both its offensive and defensive postures.

In addition to being a year of consolidation of the previous
year's gains and their exploitation, 1969 was a year of disengagement. The war in Southeast Asia had become an emotional

64

and physical drain on the American people. No longer were they content to shoulder the major economic and military burdens which they considered to be those of the Vietnamese. In January 1969, the administration of President Richard M. Nixon took office and pledged itself to the disengagement of American troops from Vietnam and the assumption of the American military role by the South Vietnamese, who by mid-1969 possessed a capable military structure. In pursuance with stated policy, the American government initiated the gradual withdrawal of American combat units. The first major Marine ground unit in I Corps to be withdrawn was Regimental Landing Team-9. On 16 July the forward echelon of RLT-9 and the 2d Battalion, 12th Marines embarked on transports for redeployment to Okinawa. By 14 August, the transfer of 2/12 was completed and the battalion took up residence at Camp Hague, Okinawa.

The area of operation remained relatively quiet during the remainder of August and September as the three remaining battalions of the 12th Marines supported combat operations of the 3d Marine Division. In mid-September, however, the entire division received orders to commence stand down operations in preparation for its transfer from Vietnam. The 1st Battalion, 12th Marines on 21 September completed its support of Operation IDAHO CANYON, and stood down along with the 3d Marines for embarkation and redeployment. Nine days later the administrative control of the 1st Battalion passed to the 3d Marines and the battalion prepared to redeploy to Camp Pendleton, California. Prior to departure, the 1st Battalion was cut to cadre strength, as most of its personnel were transferred to the 3d and 4th Battalions, 12th Marines. Following its arrival at Camp Pendleton, the 1st Battalion remained at cadre strength until 30 October when the 3d Battalion, 13th Marines was disbanded and personnel shifted to 1/12, bringing that unit up to authorized strength. (174)

Following the departure of the 1st Battalion, the remaining two battalions began displacing from forward fire support bases to larger coastal combat bases. During the period 19 October to 6 December, all the remaining units of the regiment embarked on board amphibious ships or military aircraft for transfer to Camp Hanson, Okinawa. The 3d Battalion began embarkation on 23 October and completed its redeployment on 6 December. On the morning of 5 November, a detachment of Battery M/4/12 expended the last artillery round fired by the 12th Marines in Vietnam and returned to the Dong Ha Combat Base where it was reduced to zero strength. The following day, the 4th Battalion turned over Camp Romanelli to the 2d ARVN Regiment and moved to Dong Ha where it began embarkation preparations. By 6 December the transfer of the 12th Marines from Vietnam was completed.

The conflict in Vietnam brought about a number of changes in the equipment and weaponry of the 12th Marines. The most notable change was the phasing out of the 107mm mortar or

65

howtar.(175) In the early sixties, the howtar was seen as the answer to the artillerymen's dream. It was a "helicopter-transportable, high trajectory weapon that could almost go anywhere a Marine could and deliver a round with more punch than a 105mm howitzer."(176) However, as the years progressed the howtar's liabilities(177) became more apparent and the 4.2-inch mortar was reinstituted. The same could be said of the M109 155mm howitzer (self-propelled). With the evolution of both the Marine Corps helicopter lift capabilities and the concepts of mobile artillery, the towed 155mm howitzer became a weapon that was easily transported to isolated fire bases, in contrast with the M109 which was not. The only weapon to remain unchanged was the 105mm howitzer, which again proved to be the most reliable, thus retaining its place as the Marines' basic artillery weapon. In addition to the changes in weaponry, two changes in equipment took place during the Vietnam involvement. The first was the Field Artillery Digital Computer which proved to be a highly accurate, reliable means of computing firing data, thus drastically reducing reaction time. The second change in equipment was the introduction of a new family of radios (PRC-25 series) which replaced the PRC-9 series, and increased the regiment's communications reliability. These changes in both equipment and weaponry had the effect of further improving the 12th Marines combat efficiency.

The primary concern of the 12th Marines in Vietnam was the support of Allied operations. Notwithstanding this basic role, artillerymen of the 12th engaged in an auxiliary war--the war to win the confidence of the Vietnamese people. As an important aspect of the Marine Corps' balanced approach to combat activities in Vietnam, civic action began almost immediately upon the regiment's arrival. The major emphasis of the regiment's civic action effort was concentrated on the Medical Civic Action Program (MEDCAP), as medical personnel from the regiment made numerous visits to villages surrounding established artillery positions and treated civilians for disease and wounds. The regiment also supplied the local populace with clothing, toilet articles, fertilizer, cooking oil, and school supplies, in addition to furnishing personnel to aid villagers in the construction and rehabilitation of homes, schools, churches, aid stations, and wells in an effort to improve living conditions. Similarly, the regiment supplied personnel who taught rudimentary subjects including English in local elementary and high schools. Though civic action was not the main thrust of the 12th Marines activities in Vietnam and often suffered at the expense of tactical commitments, the program proved to be advantageous to both the artillerymen and the Vietnamese people.

66

Conclusion(178)

Following its departure from Vietnam, the 12th Marines minus the 1st Battalion(179) was once more based on Okinawa--reoccupying those camps from which it departed in 1965. Its mission--to support the 3d Marine Division and to be prepared to meet a wide variety of assignments--from Japan and Korea in the North, to the Indian Ocean in the South--as part of the ready landing force of the Seventh Fleet.

Since the redeployment of the 12th Marines in December 1969, its role has changed from one of a line combat unit to that of a supporting element of the nation's force-in-readiness in the Western Pacific. As such, the regiment provides batteries for the battalion landing teams which constitute the two special landing forces of the Seventh Fleet. This reorientation has thus placed the major emphasis on extensive field training for amphibious operations. Accordingly, elements of the regiment have participated in several division and multi-national training exercises. One such operation occurred during the period 19 April-29 May 1970, when the 2d Battalion, 12th Marines joined with the 11th Marine Expeditionary Brigade in Operation GOLDEN DRAGON, a combined U.S./South Korean amphibious landing exercise. In addition to amphibious training exercises, and field firing exercises conducted on Okinawa and at Camp Fuji, Japan, artillery-men of the regiment have participated in extensive classroom training in fire direction techniques, survey, meteorology, and electronic warfare. Total preparedness was again the regiment's goal, and extensive, aggressive training was the means by which this goal was to be achieved.

Though younger than many regiments, the 12th Marines has proven its ability to respond to crisis situations in both war and peace. Should future events threaten the security of the United States or its Allies, the regiment will be ready to undertake any assignment if called upon, and accomplish it with the professionalism that has been its trademark.

67